This Book Is A Gift
to the

Library
of
Lincoln Christian
College
by

J.K. and Edna Mae Stevens

In Memory of
Christina (Christy)
Leann Morris

CHILDREN

WITHOUT

CHILDHOOD

The Playgroup Book

The Baby Reader

The Plug-In Drug:
Television, Children, and
the Family

CHILDREN

MARIE WINN

WITHOUT

PANTHEON BOOKS

CHILDHOOD

NEW YORK

All rights reserved under International and Pan-American Copyright Conventions. Published in the United States by Pantheon Books, a division of Random House, Inc., New York, and simultaneously in Canada by Random House of Canada Limited, Toronto.

A portion of this work appeared previously, in slightly different form, in *The New York Times Magazine*, January 25, 1981.

Grateful acknowledgment is made to the following for permission to reprint previously published material:

Kathryn Watterson Burkhart: Excerpt from *Growing into Love: Teenagers Talk Candidly About Sex in the 1980's* by Kathryn Watterson Burkhart. Copyright © 1981 by Kathryn Watterson Burkhart. Reprinted by permission. Emerson Books, Inc.: Excerpts from *Psychoanalysis for Teachers and Parents* by Anna Freud. Copyright 1935 by Emerson Books, Inc. Reprinted by permission of Emerson Books, Inc., Verplanck, N.Y. Families Anonymous, Inc.: Excerpts from *Families Anonymous Credo*. Copyright © 1980 by Families Anonymous, Inc. Reprinted by permission of Families Anonymous, Inc. Box 528, Van Nuys, Calif. 91480. Phillip Lopate and Teachers & Writers Collaborative: Excerpt from "Chekhov for Children" by Phillip Lopate. Copyright © 1979 by Teachers & Writers Collaborative. Reprinted from *Teachers & Writers Magazine*, Winter 1979, by permission of Phillip Lopate and Teachers & Writers Collaborative. *The New York Times*: Excerpt from "Coming of Age with Judy Blume," by Joyce Maynard, December 3, 1978. Copyright © 1978 by The New York Times Company. Reprinted by permission. Charles Scribner's Sons: Excerpt from *The Magic Years* by Selma H. Fraiberg. Copyright © 1959 by Selma H. Fraiberg. Reprinted with the permission of Charles Scribner's Sons.

Library of Congress Cataloging in Publication Data

Winn, Marie.
Children without childhood.

1. Children—United States. 2. Child rearing—
United States. 3. Family—United States. 4. United
States—Social conditions. I. Title.
HQ792.U5W495 1983   305.2'3'0973   82-48951
ISBN 0-394-51136-0

Design by Susan Mitchell

Manufactured in the United States of America
First Edition

TO MY FATHER AND MOTHER,
WITH LOVE

Contents

PART TWO

*T*HE ROOTS OF CHANGE

PREFACE

The idea that started this book sprang from my own experience as a parent. As I watched children growing up in the 1970s, my own children, my friends' children, and miscellaneous neighborhood kids, it struck me that something was fundamentally different about them —their everyday demeanor, their language, the things they knew and openly talked about. The idea that something fundamental had also changed in society's view of children and childhood came to me gradually, in the course of the hundreds of interviews I conducted for this book. As I spoke informally and at great length with the parents, doctors, and educators who generously shared their time and thoughts with me, an attitude began to emerge that surprised me and made me uneasy. It forms the heart of this book.

Since I live in New York City, my first imperative in studying patterns of change was to branch out, to talk to adults and children in other geographical locations, in suburban and rural areas and in smaller cities. I focused on two diverse communities for extensive interviews. I chose Denver, Colorado, for its Midwestern location and for its nearby isolated mountain area where I might find a more rural population. Since I had once lived in Denver, I was able to make easy contact with a large and varied parent-child network. Scotia, New York, a small suburban area outside Schenectady, I chose for its cozy, small-town feeling, and also because my cousin Helen is a fourth-grade teacher there. This gave me a fortunate access to yet another large network of parents, teachers, and children. In both communities I organized group interviews with children within the public school system, as well as a great number of individual talks with parents, teachers, school administrators, librarians, and child experts. All unattributed quotations in the following pages are taken from these interviews. I have chosen to protect all the parents and children quoted by not using their real names. But virtually every child I interviewed was openly disappointed when I told them of this decision. I promised that I would at least include their names in an acknowledgment section, which I have done.

I made no effort to achieve socioeconomic balance in these interviews—the scope of such a book would have been too unwieldy. Almost without exception the parents and children I spoke to were middle-class. But within that group I found an abundance of differences—occupational, religious, racial, political—enough variety to lead me to believe I was drawing upon a representative selection of that vital part of the American population, average American parents and children.

At the start of my investigations more than three years ago, I fully expected to find great geographical differences in the behavior patterns I was looking into. Indeed, I was prepared to discover that the precocity, the worldliness, the sophistication I had observed among children in my own community were strictly an urban phenomenon, perhaps even more specifically a New York City feature. Children in other parts of the country, I imagined, might be more innocent, more like old-fashioned children. I was surprised to find no such difference. I did, of course, come across an unworldly child here and there, one who still played with toys and read fairy tales. I also met up with some traditional kinds of parents who still dealt with children in the old familiar ways I remembered from my own childhood. But whether children were precocious or innocent seemed to relate far more to family structure and work patterns than to geographic location or community size. That is, the crucial determinant had more to do with whether the parents were divorced and whether they both worked full-time than with any other variable. It soon became apparent to me that the great social changes that have set in during the last two decades have been far more influential in changing relations between adults and children and defining children's position in society than any possible regional difference. In addition, the homogenizing influence of television has helped erase any geographical diversity that may have existed in the past.

I would like to give special thanks to Peggy Steinfels, Allan Miller, Mike and Steve Miller, Bonnie Thron, Joan Winn, and Joseph Mitchell, who read parts of the manuscript, and to Sarah Kahn, Karla Kuskin, Janet Malcolm, Helen Steiner, Joel Solomon, Betty Greene, and Aaron Green for their help and encouragement, and to Jeanne Morton of Pantheon, the copy editor of this book.

Acknowledgment is due to C. Christian Beels, M.D., Kay Brover, Ellie Caulkins, Glenn Collins, Michael I. Cohen, M.D., Vincent Crapanzano, Anne Durrell, Anke Erhardt, M.D., Richard Heffner, Karen Hein, M.D., Annie Herman, Paulina Kernberg, M.D., Jane Kramer, Milton Levine, M.D., Phillip Lopate, Maggie Mandel, Peter Neubauer, M.D., Holcolm Noble, Sarah Paul, Katharine Rees, Betsy Ross, Richard Routhier, Nora Sayre, Peter Steinfels, Charlotte Zolotow.

M. Aragon, Rabbi Joshua Bakst, William Branch, Doris Burns, Geraldine Cook, Donna Coombs, Marty DelMonaco, Helen Dillon, Shirley Early, Norma Giron, Albert Goetz, Emily Graham, Pat Hayes, Mary Ann Hull, Francie Joslin, Dick Koeppe, Bob Korthas, John Kuntz, Rosemary Lawless, Lucy Lawson, Theada McIlvenny, Linda Metcalfe, Nancy Migneault, Joanne Milavek, Jack Nelson, Ruth Ritterband, Rita Romeo, Maureen Sauter, Randy Testa, Mamie Toll, Joann Welch, Barbara Wurz, Hillel Zaremba.

Ginny Avery, Maja Bednarski, Lisa Berg, Jean Bundy, Lillie Burrell, Martha Cox, Midge Cullen, Cathy Currin, Helen Donadio, Sophia Duckworth, Carole George, Vesna Gjaja, Terri Glynn, Mona Goldenberg, Beth Griffiths, Mary Lou deGuire, Mary Hannahs, Nancy Haugen, Diane Hebert, Tina and David Hinkley, Marcia Johnson, Sharon Jones, Cindy Kahn, Shirley Kinzele, Kent and Liz Kreider, Marlene Lederer, Carolyn Lewis, Gail Lipson, Clara Longstreth, Linda McKnight, Barbara Moe, Barbara Nathanson, Anne O'Sul-

livan, Dave Petricca, Florence Phillips, Nancy Pike, Linda Pom-
merer, Fern Portnoy, Marie Prentice, Sandy and Bob Rhodes, Steve
Rosenfeld, Ann Shafer, Donna Singer, Fred and Mareline Staub,
Caroline and Harry Subin, Arlin Sutherland, Mary Ann Undrill,
Irene Uzgiras, Florence Walker, Becky Weaver, Elaine Wertalik,
Jean Zegger

And finally, thanks to the kids:
Lisa Abeel, Amy Adams, Barbara Adams, Amit Agrawal, Mark Alb-
right, Glenn Arnold, Abby Asher, Neal Baley, Hunky Banbury,
Sabina Bednarski, Jenny Bergstrom, Anna Berkenblit, Ted Birkey,
Kim Blakeley, Bobby Blumenfield, Jay Blumenfield, Matt Bond,
Mercer Borden, Alice Brover, Kenny Bubrmaster, Jim Burns, Mary
Caulkins, Elizabeth Cheroutes, Trisha Cognetta, Shannon Connery,
Renee Cooke, Jason Cooper, Giulia Cox, William Cox, Shelley Cul-
len, Michelle Culler, Chad Currin, Robert DellaVilla, Jennifer
Deluca, Amy Deutl, Eric Dickson, Jr., Debby D'Isabel, Dina Dona-
dio, John Early, Shannon Emery, Stefanie Feuer, Suzanne George,
Marin Gjaja, Paul Glynn, Nisha Goel, Diana Goldberg, Jeff
Griffiths, Alexandra Guarnaschelli, Steve Gutterman, Carol Han-
nahs, Sheila Harbin, Jenny Harris, Mellissa Hart, Rachel Hart, Tyler
Harvey, Paul Heiner, Jonathan Hinkley, Jennifer Hobins, Julie
Holt, David Kahn, John Kahn, Gail Katz, Andy Kingsley, Sarah
Kreider, Doug Lapp, David Lee, Michael Lewis, Debbie Lilley,
Horst deLorenzi, Chris Loux, Sherri McGrail, Karen McKnight,
Peter McLaughlin, Ingrid Medelman, Mark Messenbaugh, David
Michael, Heiner Mohnen, Monique Moyse, Sue Ness, Lara Noonan,
Christine O'Connor, Sean O'Keefe, Scott Olinger, Mark O'Sullivan,
Darnell Parker, Kim Percent, Leah Pike, Emily Polachek, Eric Pom-
merer, James Powers, Laurie Rankin, Mindy Reilly, Lis Reinstein,
Kate Reppel, Frank Rispoli, Sonia Savkar, Sunil Savkar, Edna
Scheindling, Nina Shafer, Susannah Sheffer, Kenny Shihrer, Allison
Simpson, Tara Simsak, Mike Singer, Christine Smith, Debbie Smith,
Lisa Smith, Tahlia Spector, Amy Stankevich, Gordon Stanton, Phil-
lip Staub, Gabrielle Steinfels, John Melville Steinfels, Pam Stewart,
Samantha Strauss, Dave Susich, Sarah Taggart, Howard Tanner,

Nicki Undrill, Rimas Uzgiras, Regan Vann, Beth van Dewater, Page Volean, John Walstrom, Sten Walstrom, Elaine Weiner, Annette Wertalik, Gina Wertalik, Louis John Wertalik, Susie Wheeler, Linda Ann Wicks, Mike Wilson, Jane Wulf, Lisa Zegger, Nina Zegger.

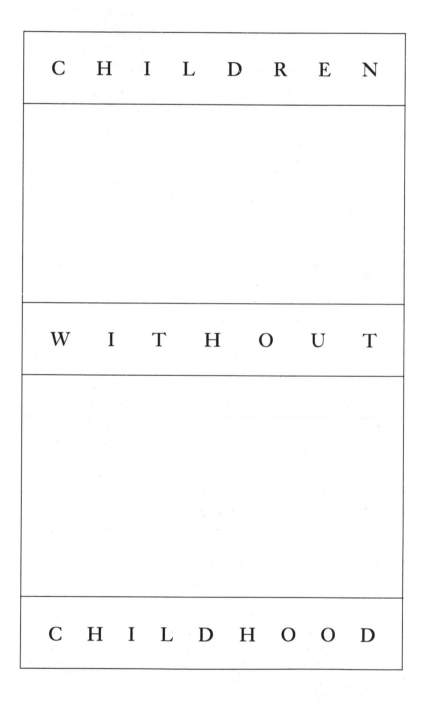

C H I L D R E N

W I T H O U T

C H I L D H O O D

SOMETHING HAS HAPPENED

O nce upon a time a fictional twelve-year-old from New England named Lolita Haze slept with a middle-aged European intellectual named Humbert Humbert and profoundly shocked American sensibilities. It was not so much the idea of an adult having sexual designs on a child that was appalling. It was Lolita herself, unvirginal long before Humbert came upon the scene, Lolita, so knowing, so jaded, so *unchildlike*, who seemed to violate something America held sacred. The book was banned in Boston. Even a sophisticated book reviewer of the *New York Times* called Nabokov's novel "repulsive" and "disgusting."

No more than a single generation after *Lolita*'s publication Nabokov's vision of American childhood seems prophetic. There is little doubt that schoolchildren of the 1980s are more akin to Nabokov's nymphet than to those guileless and innocent creatures with their shiny Mary Janes and pigtails, their scraped knees and trusting ways, that were called children not so long ago.

Something has happened to the joys of childhood. The child of a generation ago, observes the satirical magazine *National Lampoon*, spent his typical Saturday afternoon "climbing around a construction site, jumping off a garage roof and onto an old sofa, having a crabapple war, mowing the lawn." The agenda for today's child, however, reads: "Sleep late, watch TV, tennis lesson, go to shopping mall and buy albums and new screen for bong, play electronic WW II, watch TV, get high." The bulging pockets of the child of the past are itemized: "knife, compass, 36¢, marble, rabbit's foot." The contemporary tot's pocket, on the other hand, contains "hash pipe, Pop Rocks, condom, $20.00, 'ludes, Merits."[1]

Something has happened to the limits of childhood. An advertisement for a new line of books called "Young Adult Books" defines a young adult as "a person facing the problems of adulthood."[2] The books, however, which deal with subjects such as prostitution, divorce, and rape, are aimed at readers between the ages of ten and thirteen, "persons" who were formerly known as children.

Something has happened to the image of childhood. A full-page advertisement in a theatrical newspaper showing a sultry female wearing dark lipstick, excessive eye-shadow, a mink coat, and possibly nothing else bears the legend: "Would you believe I'm only ten?" We believe it. For beyond the extravagances of show business lies the evidence of a population of normal, regular children, once clearly distinguishable as little boys and little girls, who now look and act like little grown-ups.

Something has happened to blur the formerly distinct boundaries between childhood and adulthood, to weaken the protective membrane that once served to shelter children from precocious experience and sorrowful knowledge of the adult world. All over the country newly single mothers are sitting down with their children and making what has come to be known as The Speech: "Look, things are going to have to be different. We're all in this together and we're going to have to be partners." Things truly are different for great numbers of children today as the traditional, hierarchical structure of the family in which children are children and parents are adults is eroded and new partnerships are forged.

What's going on with children today? Is everything happening too soon? There is nothing wrong with sex, the modern adult has come to understand well, but what about sex at age twelve? Marijuana and alcohol are common social accessories in today's society, but is sixth grade the right time to be introduced to their gratifications? Should nine-year-olds have to worry about homosexuality? Their parents hardly knew the word until their teens. Lassitude, indifference, cynicism, are understandable defenses against the hardships of modern adult life, but aren't these states antithetical to childhood? Shouldn't these kids be out at the old fishing hole or playing with their dolls or stamp albums instead of reading *Screw* and *Hustler,* or flicking the TV dial to see what's playing, just like weary adults after a hard day's work? Shouldn't childhood be special and different?

We are at the beginnings of a new era, and like every time of transition from one way of thinking to another, ours is characterized by resistance, anxiety, and no small amount of nostalgia for those familiar landmarks that most contemporary adults still recall from their own "old-era" childhoods. And yet the change has occurred so swiftly that most adults are hardly aware that a true conceptual and behavioral revolution is under way, one that has yet to be clearly defined and understood. At the heart of the matter lies a profound alteration in society's attitude towards children. Once parents struggled to preserve children's innocence, to keep childhood a carefree golden age, and to shelter children from life's vicissitudes. The new era operates on the belief that children must be exposed early to adult experience in order to survive in an increasingly complex and uncontrollable world. The Age of Protection has ended. An Age of Preparation has set in.

Every aspect of contemporary children's lives is affected by this change in the way adults think about children. Indeed, it is a change as consequential as the transformation in thinking and behaving that occurred at the end of the Middle Ages. Not until then was childhood recognized as a distinct entity and children perceived as special creatures with special needs, not miniature versions of adults. Today's integration of children into adult life marks a curious return to that old, undifferentiated state of affairs in which childhood and adulthood were merged into one.

To be sure, today's changed approach to children did not result from some deliberate adult decision to treat kids in a new way; it developed out of necessity. For children's lives are always a mirror of adult life. The great social upheavals of the late 1960s and early 1970s—the so-called sexual revolution, the women's movement, the proliferation of television in American homes and its larger role in child rearing and family life, the rampant increase in divorce and single parenthood, political disillusionment in the Vietnam and post-Vietnam era, a deteriorating economic situation that propels more mothers into the work force—all these brought about changes in adult life that necessitated new ways of dealing with children.

No single societal change, however important, can account for the end of a centuries-old conviction about childhood and the emergence of a brave new relationship between adults and children. It was the confluence of all these changes at one time, acting upon each other and upon society as a whole, that helped to alter long-established patterns within the course of a single decade. Only with the rise in two-career families and only with the mounting divorce rate, two factors to come up again and again in the course of this discussion, did parents have cause to withdraw their close, protective attention from children. Only with the fascinating presence of television in every home, mesmerizing and sedating normally unpredictable and demanding children, was the actual decrease in adult attention and supervision made possible. This conjunction occurred in the 1960s. Suddenly the idea of childhood as a special and protected condition came to seem inadvisable if not actually dangerous, and in any event, quite impossible to maintain.

Which came first, the unchildlike child or the unprotecting adult? There is an intricate interconnection to be found between society's underlying concepts of childhood and children's perceivable behavior. A circular pattern always comes into view. For instance, as today's children impress adults with their sophisticated ways, adults begin to change their ideas about children and their needs; that is, they form new conceptions of childhood. Why, these tough little customers don't require protection and careful nurture! No longer need adults withhold information about the harsh realities of life from children. No longer need they hide the truth about their own weaknesses. Rather, they begin to feel it is their duty to prepare children for the exigencies of modern life. However, as adults act less protectively (not entirely as a reaction to the seeming worldliness of their children, of course, but also because of their own adult concerns, their work, their marital problems) and as they expose children to the formerly secret underside of their lives—adult sexuality, violence, injustice, suffering, fear of death—those former innocents grow tougher, perforce, less playful and trusting, more skeptical—in short, more like adults. We have come full circle.

This book is about those unchildlike children and about their newly unprotected position in today's changing society. The first part examines the realities of the present shift from a protective to a preparatory approach to children: the sense parents have that they cannot control what happens to their kids; the shrinking boundaries between children and adults as adult authority declines and children's respect for their elders becomes a thing of the past; the new openness of adults to children and children to adults, as children are let into once hidden territories of adult life; the influence of television on children's free time, and especially its role in eliminating play from children's lives.

The second part considers the historical antecedents of the change, how concepts of childhood and children's consequent position in society have altered over the centuries. This section includes a look at a new kind of child rearing and a discussion of two crucial societal changes that underlie children's new integration into adult life: notably, the new position of women in society, and the rampantly unstable condition of marriage today.

The third section considers the impact of sexual acceleration on childhood and presents, from various points of view, thoughts on the broader purpose of a prolonged period of protection and innocence at the beginning of life.

PART

*F*ROM

PROTECTION

TO

PREPARATION

ONE

Out-of-control Parents

THE PEARL HARBOR METHOD

In the Golden Age of Childhood, parents rarely worried that their school-age children would get into any serious trouble in their hours away from home. The kids were pretty well in hand, parents believed, even the most stubborn and independent of the lot. A child might come to grief by breaking a window with a baseball or flunking a test in school or, at the worst, getting caught in a minor infraction such as sneaking into the movies or lifting a candy bar. Parents agonized over these problems, worrying that their son or daughter wouldn't get into college, wouldn't have the sort of moral fiber it takes to grow up to be President. But apart from the inevitable anxieties about sickness or accidents, mothers and fathers felt confident that nothing untoward was likely to happen in the course of their children's daily lives. Never in their worst fantasies did they imagine that their ten- or eleven-year-olds might smoke dope or get involved in serious sexual activity or run away from home and fall into the clutches of a child-prostitution ring. Parents then hardly knew that a drug called marijuana existed, much less feared that junior-high-school-age children might want to get high on it. As for child prostitution and the like—why, that sort of thing might go on in Tangier or the Casbah, but not around here!

To be sure, even in the past, as their children approached the middle years of adolescence, parents' sense of being in control began to weaken. Suddenly those formerly docile boys and girls, tractable even in the moody years of early adolescence, were taking real risks. They passed their drivers' tests and risked their lives in cars. They experimented with alcohol, making their hours behind the wheel even more dangerous. They certainly began to get involved in some form of sexual activity, sometimes running the risk of getting pregnant or getting someone else pregnant. Parents tore their hair and complained bitterly about how impossible it all was. But in fact, everybody agreed that these children were *not really children.* Practically adult in physical development, perched on the edge of the domestic nest, so to speak, they only had a year or two to go before they took off on their own, either for college, for the army, or for the world of work. Though they might remain semidependent family members for many years after, nevertheless they would never again be considered family *children.*

Today, not long after the end of early childhood, with many years of shared family life looming ahead, parents are faced with the knowledge that their young children *can* get involved in any number of dangerous, illegal, or merely unsuitable activities. Short of locking the kids up in their rooms, or establishing family rules that are wildly out of whack with community standards (such as "No visiting other children's homes"), parents know there isn't much they can do to keep their children from doing whatever they want, especially if other kids are doing it too. Today twelve-year-olds *do* become potheads, *do* have sexual intercourse, *do* watch pornographic films on television, *do* get involved in any number of unchildlike activities. Yet they have years to go before they are no longer considered children, before they can legally try to make it on their own.

Not all children, it is clear, get into trouble these days. There are still those who wouldn't dream of smoking a joint or doing anything mushy with a member of the opposite sex. Many pre-teenagers persist in reading E. Nesbit and Noel Streatfeild rather than Judy Blume and Paul Zindel; there are others whose idea of a good time at the movies is to see Lassie, not Caligula. Indeed, statistically speaking, the number of preadolescents seriously involved in drugs, alcohol, and sex remains relatively small. Furthermore, the incidence of these problems is far higher in troubled families than in stable ones.

But virtually no parents today are spared a feeling of being out of control of their children's lives. Precocity seems catching, somehow, like head lice: the nicest kids fall prey to it. In their fearful knowledge of what childhood holds in store for some children, parents cannot be sure what lies ahead for their own. Ignorance truly *was* bliss, once upon a time.

A skit presented recently on the popular satirical program *Saturday Night Live* points out the grave dilemma parents face when they feel out of control. In the mock drama, two obstetricians in operating-room greens are being interviewed by a talk-show host. The first doctor is a spokesman for the Leboyer childbirth method. He advocates that doctors make a supreme effort to bring the newborn into the world without undue shock or trauma, and then demonstrates his technique. The lights are turned down low. The delivery room personnel smile, speak in soft, melodious voices. As the baby emerges it is not spanked; rather, it is tenderly placed on the mother's stomach. She and the doctor gently caress it. Then, before the umbilical cord is severed, the baby is bathed in warm water in an effort to approximate the environment of the amniotic fluid within the womb. Thus, doctor number one believes, the child is given a good start in life.

The second doctor announces that he represents a very different point of view, though he too expects to make the experience of birth advantageous for the child's future. His method is called the Pearl Harbor method. Using a large doll to represent the newborn, the doctor snatches the baby roughly as it emerges into the world. Then, as the assistants shout and scream and set off firecrackers, he tosses the baby in the air, spanks it, and proceeds to run interference with it in an improvised football game in the delivery room. The idea, the doctor explains, is "to get the baby used to the difficult new world it will have to live in as soon as possible."

As today's parents look around with anxiety and confusion at a society amazingly different from the one they grew up in, a world far less innocent and safe and secure, they fear they can no longer shelter their children from life's dangers. They turn instead to a new, Pearl Harbor style of child rearing: they prepare rather than protect.

T H E   M Y T H   O F   T H E   T E E N A G E   W E R E W O L F

A pervasive myth has taken hold of parents' imagination these days, contributing to their feeling of being powerless to control the fates of their children: the myth of the teenage werewolf. Its message is that no matter how pleasant and sweet and innocent their child might be at the moment, how amiable and docile and friendly, come the first hormonal surge of puberty and the child will turn into an uncontrollable monster. But unlike the lycanthrope who turns harmless at the next day's sunrise, the teenage werewolf, belief has it, remains monstrous for years and years. It is a terrible myth that darkens the years of parenthood.

In her novel *The War Between the Tates*, Alison Lurie describes the dread metamorphosis:

> They were a happy family once, she thinks. Jeffrey and Matilda were beautiful, healthy babies; charming toddlers; intelligent, lively, affectionate children. There are photograph albums and folders of drawings and stories and report cards to prove it. Then last year, when Jeffrey turned fourteen and Matilda twelve, they had begun to change; to grow rude, coarse, selfish, insolent, nasty, brutish, and tall. It was as if she were keeping a boarding house in a bad dream, and the children she had loved were turning into awful lodgers—lodgers who paid no rent, whose leases could not be terminated. They were awful at home and abroad; in company and alone; in the morning, the afternoon and the evening. . . .
>
> Though equally awful, the children are awful in somewhat different ways. Jeffrey is sullen, restless and intermittently violent. Matilda is sulky, lazy and intermittently dishonest. Jeffrey is obsessed with inventions and space; Matilda with clothes and pop music. Matilda is extravagant and wasteful; Jeffrey miserly and

ungenerous. Jeffrey is still doing all right in school, while his sister's grades are hopeless. . . .¹

Everyone has heard similar tales. And the metamorphosis seems to happen earlier and earlier. As the years of childhood go on, parents steel their nerves and wait for the sword to descend, for their family life to disintegrate. Even parents of infants and preschoolers find their relationships with their children affected by the teenage-werewolf myth.

"I see the reality of my kids now," says the father of a seven-year-old and a three-year-old, "beautiful, wonderful, innocent, childlike creatures, and I think of the stereotypical fantasy of the bombed-out adolescent, giggling on the phone, smoking pot, snarling at parents —I can hardly stand to think of it. I feel I have to back away a little, not get too emotionally involved."

Parents of the past, to be sure, expected a little trouble when their children reached adolescence. They knew they would face some rebelliousness, some painful disharmony. But the idea that children at puberty or before would be transformed into frightening and uncontrollable presences did not capture the public imagination until the last decade or so. What gave rise to this new image?

A part of the answer may be found in the drug epidemic of the 1960s. Some of the drug horror stories that were widely circulated in the late sixties and early seventies continue to haunt today's parents. As an uneasy mother explains, "Drugs is the area I'm most terrified about. We know a couple of really monstrous teenagers just wasted from drugs who were formerly really nice little kids we loved and spent a lot of time with. I'm dreading that this sort of thing might happen to our nice, well-behaved little boys."

In the same way a New York father pinpoints the source of his fears that his young children will turn overnight into ravening beasts. "I know adolescents have to rebel," he says, "I was quite a rebellious teenager myself. But it was much more innocent in those days. It was strictly a style-and-culture sort of rebellion. I wore engineer boots and a leather jacket. I wore my hair in a DA and I listened to rock-and-roll. My parents couldn't stand any of it. But we didn't have drugs. The potential for getting wrecked with drugs is so great. All those drug stories and documentaries on TV make it terribly clear that it's much more dangerous to be a teenager today."

A typical drug story, one of hundreds that feed the fears of parents throughout America, is *Ellen: A Mother's Story of Her Runaway Daughter*, by Betty Wason, published in the 1970s. The book also gives a brief account of thirteen-year-old Stephanie, once "a popular girl, bright, a conscientious student, active in sports, 'well adjusted' by all the usual criteria," who was found dead in her bedroom in Springfield, Virginia, one morning in March, after she had soaked a wad of paper with aerosol spray and held it under her nose to inhale. The autopsy also showed that she had been smoking marijuana the preceding afternoon, although her parents declared, "We had no idea that she had either smoked marijuana, experimented with aerosol or used any other hairy [*sic*] substances."[2] A typical teenage-werewolf story.

In reality the teenage werewolf *is* a myth: the number of pre-teenagers or early adolescents who become seriously involved with drugs represents a small fraction of the age group—4 percent of twelve-year-olds, according to a 1977 survey. Nevertheless, the very existence of the problem creates deep anxiety among parents, and the media play on this anxiety with venal calculation: an article or program about schoolchildren taking drugs will attract a large audience; the program will have a high rating, the magazine will sell well. Thus an article about head shops in the newspaper supplement *Parade*[3] is illustrated with a posed photograph of a boy who cannot be older than nine holding a water pipe, surrounded by drug paraphernalia, looking stoned.

Yet it is not anxiety alone that has made parents in America believe in the teenage-werewolf myth. During the last several decades there have been signs among adults of an increasing ambivalence if not outright hostility towards children. Consider the changing image of children in the movies. In the sixties a new sort of child appeared in motion pictures; from a sweet, idealized Shirley Temple or Margaret O'Brien poppet, the movie child grew into a monster. First came Patty McCormack, playing a prepubescent killer in *The Bad Seed* in 1956. Then, in *Village of the Damned* (1962), sweet-faced children turned out to be malevolent beings from outer space. The trend accelerated in the late sixties and early seventies, culminating in the appearance of a spate of satanic juveniles on movie screens. *Rosemary's Baby* was the first, a mild exercise in horror compared to *The Exorcist*, which featured the first true teenage werewolf, a darling little girl transformed, just at puberty, into a ravening, sexually rapacious, and murderous creature. Twelve-year-old Linda Blair, masturbating with a crucifix while she shouts blasphemies and obscenities, may be the ultimate embodiment of that time-old endearment directed at children, "You little devil!"*

Surely there is an element of wish fulfillment in the appetite of today's adult audience for television documentaries about child abuse, child prostitution, child molestation, for screen images of children being beaten, burned, sexually debauched, or destroyed by drugs, as well as in the popularity of those portraits of little spawns of the devil who batter parents, kill friendly neighbors, and do terrible things to themselves with religious objects.

By the same token, the widespread fear among today's parents that their manageable children will turn overnight into dope fiends, school dropouts, or voracious sexual voluptuaries reflects a certain anger and animosity towards the young, a fear and loathing that helps turn the myth into a self-fulfilling prophecy. After all, there were "bad" children and uncontrolled teenagers in the past; nevertheless, parents expected their own children to be good, to grow up well. The exceptions were called "black sheep." The fact that today's parents are amazed if their children do *not* turn into black sheep makes it clear that a less than optimistic, indeed a deeply distrustful and negative, attitude towards children exists today.

Perhaps some of the hostility underlying the myth of the teenage werewolf is related to those current child-rearing trends that emphasize democracy, equality, and shared decision making, which have

---

*It is interesting to speculate on a new wave of movies featuring children whose parents are divorcing or divorced—notably the children in *Shoot the Moon* or *Kramer vs. Kramer*, the child in *Close Encounters of the Third Kind*, and the children in *E.T., the Extra-Terrestrial*. These kids are not at all monstrous. They are lovable. Perhaps they have been punished enough for being children in this era by the loss of a parent and a stable family.

helped produce children who are often more difficult to live with than their more repressed counterparts of the past and who may in consequence engender murderous wishes in their parents.

Or perhaps the teenage-werewolf myth is a projection of the parents' guilt at pursuing their own narcissistic aims of "self-fulfillment." Instead of being willing as a society to sacrifice for children, to consider their care a primary duty, adults have transformed the very image of childhood from one that deserves protection and nurture to one that justifies their own sometimes monstrous abandonment of children.

"SEXUALLY ACTIVE" CHILDREN

If ignorance was bliss for parents of the past, it may be that a little bit of knowledge is a dangerous thing for parents of the present. For a certain distortion, presenting children as far more precocious and depraved than they really are, has appeared in the popular perception of children that is creating uneasiness among parents. This distortion, by affecting child-rearing styles, may very well encourage those very forms of behavior that parents fear most.

Consider an odd phenomenon: parents of twelve- or thirteen-year-old girls rarely answer "Of course" today when asked if their daughters are virgins, even when to an outside observer the daughter in question appears obviously undeveloped—flat-chested, squeaky-voiced, and barely pubertal. Somehow people have come to believe that ever since the sexual revolution, with its loosening of sexual standards, the majority of young adolescents become sexually active not long after the onset of puberty. Puberty, after all, spells the commencement of reproductive capacity. Therefore, the belief has it, when the social barriers to sexual expression are removed, then, like young people on some South Sea Island in the old anthropology books or geographic magazines, twelve- and thirteen-year-olds in great numbers will be happily casting off the shackles of an outmoded Victorian morality to "have sex," as they say, at every opportunity.

The juxtaposition of this common impression of early sexuality with the reality of an average classroom of contemporary seventh- or eighth-graders is startling. In spite of their nonchildish clothing, their Farrah Fawcett or punk hairdos, their "cool" use of sexual expletives in ordinary conversation, the idea of these kids having sexual intercourse seems so out of line with their manifest immaturity as to make us wonder whether something hasn't radically changed about the sexual act itself.

The prevailing view of early adolescence as a time of heightened sexuality springs partially from the use of children and young adolescents as sex objects by the media. The steady stream of barely pubescent girls being raped on soap operas, sleeping with their fathers in best-selling novels, and looking sultry and postcoital in magazine ads has undoubtedly contributed to the new image of the sexual child. In imitating these sexy role models in their carriage and demeanor, real fifth-through-eighth-graders acquire certain mannerisms of dress and behavior that add to their parents' uncertainty about what they're up to sexually.

The belief in extensive sexual precocity among pre-teenagers and teenagers these days may also be traced to certain well-publicized statistics about sexuality. There is, for instance, the dramatically increased number of teenagers having illegitimate babies during the last twenty years. Most people assume that this automatically proves teenagers are also more sexually active now—after all, you have to "do it" to get pregnant. But the authors of the study *Teenage Sexuality, Pregnancy and Childbearing*[4] have an alternative explanation. They propose that the teenager who became pregnant two decades ago was far more likely to legitimate her baby by getting married than today's teenager for whom illegitimacy no longer bears the same stigma. Statistics gathered by the authors of the study confirm this hypothesis: great numbers of babies born to teenage mothers in the 1950s and 1960s followed within seven or eight months of marriage. Perhaps a few of these babies were premature, but most of the weddings it is clear, were helped along by a "shotgun." Seen from this perspective, a rise in teenage pregnancies does not necessarily prove a huge increase in teenage sexual activity.

There has, to be sure, been a loosening of sexual standards in society as a whole. And many parents are familiar with a reliable survey by Zelnick and Kantner[5] revealing that the proportion of teenagers who are "sexually active" has increased substantially in the last decade. But even this statistic is misleading. The term "sexually active" inevitably leads to images of sexual prowess, if not athleticism, just as the term "physically active" suggests someone who jogs every day, does push-ups, and generally engages in regular physical activity. But the children defined as "sexually active" in these studies are simply those who have had sexual intercourse at least once, and there is no way to judge for how many of them it was only once. Indeed, further research shows that there has been a *decrease* in frequency of intercourse among teenagers in recent years. What is more, over half the teenagers dubbed "sexually active" in the survey had had no intercourse in the month prior to the survey. Thus, in reality, more than half of them might realistically be called sexually *in*active, that is, *rarely* sexually active. Yet studies like these nourish the public perception of rampant teenage sexuality: if 34.9 percent of a sample between the ages of fifteen and nineteen are found to be "sexually active," then it is assumed there must be a great deal of sexual activity among teenagers generally.

An alternative explanation for the seeming increase in "sexual activity" among teenagers is that young people today no longer value the notion of premarital chastity and may be willing to engage in sexual experiments at earlier ages and outside marriage. Sex may well be a less important, more casual part of their lives than it was of the lives of teenagers twenty or more years ago. Perhaps when sex is not a forbidden fruit, it loses some of its deliciousness for the rebellious young. Moreover, the new assertiveness and feminism of today's young females may lead to less sexual activity than in the past; they may lose their virginity earlier than their counterparts of the fifties or sixties—sometimes out of sheer curiosity—but they are less likely to be pressured into further sexual experiences with males whose adolescent sex drive is often stronger than their own.

The upshot of the pervasive public belief in the uncontrollable sexuality of teenagers, and even of pre-teenagers, is that parents are half-hearted in their efforts to supervise and control their children, even when they are filled with anxiety as to their children's ability to cope with a full-fledged sexual relationship. "How can we buck the tide?" parents say helplessly, often without making quite certain that the ocean they see is a real one and not a mirage.

FEAR OF RUNAWAYS

In trying to understand the pervasive feeling of helplessness that overcomes so many parents today, we may trace some of their anxiety to a particularly chilling phenomenon of the 1960s, the runaway epidemic.

A New York mother described her inability to control her thirteen-year-old daughter's comings and goings at night: "This year Sandy and her little pack started going out to clubs. Clubs like Xenon —you know, discos. They spend hours getting themselves done up —they know that's the only way they'll get in, if they look outrageous, so they wear all this make-up and these outlandish costumes. Honestly, they look like miniature hookers! They go out all together at about eleven P.M. and they come back all together, in cabs, at two or three in the morning, and they sleep at each other's houses. It really makes me nervous having Sandy out that late, and God knows what goes on there."

Why, then, doesn't she simply forbid her daughter to go? this mother was asked. Her answer revealed a not uncommon fear: "I *do* object to her going to clubs, but I really don't dare stop it. When you and I were growing up, when we were told to be home at midnight we came home, even if we didn't want to. But in the sixties, when parents told their kid to be home, and the kid said 'No,' and the parent made a big deal of it, well, *the kid just ran away.* Now we've had two decades of runaways, and that's always in the back of my mind. I think I've raised both my daughters so that they'd never want to run away. The pictures of those little kids hitchhiking across the country, getting raped and killed, those posters of missing kids all over the place—those have never gotten out of my mind. Every time Sandy slams the door on me and gets mad because I try to clamp down a little bit, I think that activates my fear of runaways."

In addition, the divorce epidemic has introduced a new kind of running away that children themselves use as a threat in order to wrest control from the custodial parent. "I was terribly upset when I found out my thirteen-year-old daughter was smoking marijuana regularly at parties every weekend," a divorced mother reported. "I tried everything, yelling and screaming, cajoling, bribery. Finally, when she kept coming home later and later, obviously stoned, I told her I wouldn't allow her to go out at night any more. She'd say, 'You can't stop me,' and I'd say, 'I'm going to lock you in your room if I have to. You're not going.' And so she said, 'If you do that I'll run away and go live with Daddy.' That was something I couldn't deal with. I broke down and let her go."

THE END OF SUPERVISION

At the heart of parental loss of control lies the fact that parents today supervise their school-age children less than their counterparts did even ten years and certainly twenty years ago. A new parental casualness is so much the norm these days that only when one compares contemporary children's lives with those of the 1960s and early 1970s does one realize how much earlier the parental reins are loosened today. There is clear evidence of an overall decrease in parental vigilance about every aspect of children's lives, from the trivial to the life-threatening. Indeed, so universal is children's earlier freedom in today's society that what was once seen as care and nurture is now often regarded as overprotectiveness. Today's children seem to be about two years advanced when compared with children ten years ago. Kids cross the street without holding an adult's hand at four years instead of at six. Seven-year-olds ride the bus alone where once they had to wait until they were nine or ten. Bedtime for seven-year-olds is commonly ten P.M., as it once was for fifth- or sixth-graders, while *those* "young adults"—as they are called in the publishing trade —often don't have any required bedtime at all. (A recent informal survey of fifth- and sixth-graders revealed that the majority no longer consider themselves children. When asked "What are you, then?" they answered "Pre-teenagers" or "Young adults.")

What are the reasons for this decline in child supervision? The most obvious are the rising divorce rate and the increase in two-career families. In each case the parents' attention is inevitably diverted from child supervision to adult matters. Another part of the answer may be that children today, thanks to their new precocity, are simply more difficult to supervise than children were fifteen or twenty years ago. Faced with a steady battle on their hands and with the standard "everybody else can stay out until one A.M." ploy that children have used from time immemorial, faced with kids who may be only eleven or twelve but who "talk sixteen," parents are more inclined these days to capitulate.

But at least a part of the reason school-age children receive less supervision today resides in a deterministic conviction that the die is cast during early childhood and that it doesn't much matter what parents do during the later stages. By the beginning of the 1960s such a belief came to prevail. This paved the way for a large-scale abandonment of school-age children, the very population whose unchildlike and frequently self-destructive behavior is causing so much concern today.

British psychiatrist John Bowlby was probably the first, and is to this day the most influential, figure in the conversion of American parents to a belief in the supreme importance of early childhood experience. His *Child Care and the Growth of Love*,[6] a popularized version of his scholarly study of the effects of short and long separations of infants and preschool children from their mothers, had a profound effect on American child rearing. As the devastating findings of Bowlby's study became widely known, through his own books and through the writings of other child experts who had read them, parents came to understand the terrible connection between the child's early life and its adult outcome. When Bowlby described in moving detail the grief and mourning of two-year-olds separated from their mothers for periods of time, and the permanent scars this experience left on their future ability to trust and love, American parents began to think twice about leaving their toddlers with a baby-sitter even for the evening, let alone a week's vacation. But the important corollary of Bowlby's influence was to imprint firmly in parents' minds the understanding that the child's fate was unalterably determined in those early years. Basing his conclusions firmly on Freudian principles, Bowlby graphically demonstrated to parents that it was the early years that counted above all.

The 1960s and early 1970s saw a surge of interest in early childhood. Much research was initiated in that period; virtually all of it, whether dealing with the cognitive, the emotional, or the social development of preschool children, proved to be deterministic in its conclusions. Two influential books of the sixties, Joseph McVicker Hunt's *Intelligence and Experience* and Benjamin Bloom's *Stability and Change in Human Characteristics*, stressed the fact that IQ scores in early childhood correlate with adult IQ ratings, thus strengthening the idea that the child's intellectual fate is sealed by the time he begins school. Harry Harlow's widely publicized experiments with monkeys deprived of maternal affection emphasized the vulnerability of early childhood and implied that later stages of life were more impervious to change. A further spur to early-childhood determinism was the publication of Christopher Jencks's book *Inequality* in 1972. Demonstrating that the American dream of progress through children's education was unrealistic, this widely circulated book intensified the already strong conviction that the child's fate is determined during early childhood.[7]

The practical result of early-childhood determinism is a new kind of liberation for parents: if they believe the major part of the human personality is formed before children start school, once the preschool years are over, parents don't have to worry about how much time they spend with their kids, how much they supervise their activities, how carefully they steer them in one direction or another. They simply have to provide food and clothing, pay the orthodontist's bills, and all will be well. For those beleaguered parents of the 1970s and 1980s trying to save their marriages or recover from their divorces, struggling to keep their heads above water economically, pursuing their demanding new careers, hopelessly attempting to control their children's television viewing, early-childhood determinism appeared to be a gift from the gods.

DRUGS, SEX, AND REAL CHILDREN

Independence, to be sure, is a much desired goal of child rearing, and so is self-sufficiency. Why not look upon the trend towards less supervision as a good thing? If children outside their parents' control were found to behave with maturity and to conduct their lives in constructive and wholesome ways, then surely a nation of independent twelve-year-olds would be no cause for alarm. The trouble is that some children do *not* show precocious maturity, and use their freedom to get involved in dangerous and self-destructive activities. But by the time parents recognize the danger, they have often lost control over their children and it is too late to regain it.

The connection between children's new freedom from adult supervision and their precocious experimentation with drugs and sex is underlined by a rarely remembered fact: at the very height of the "drug epidemic" of the sixties and seventies there were actually no real *children* involved. The druggies and flower-children of that difficult era were mostly college students, legitimately old enough to pursue unsupervised lives. The fifth-, sixth-, and seventh-graders were still being brought up under their parents' eagle eye. Where would those school kids have gone for illicit experimentation fifteen years ago, when most suburban homes were still complete with a domesticated mom waiting after school with milk and cookies?

The eagle eye began to defocus towards the middle of the seventies as the increase in divorce and women's employment left a vast population of unsupervised children in cities, suburbs, and rural areas around America. Now it was easy to find an empty house or apartment in which to "party," a verb children use now to refer to their periodic get-togethers at which they smoke joints and "make out" (not to be confused with the old-fashioned noun "party," with cakes and paper hats and all).

Suddenly media attention turned to "children" rather than "teen-agers" in articles and documentaries about sex and drugs. A 1980 article in *Newsweek* reported that "young people, especially, are turn-ing on to pot earlier, more often, and in greater numbers than ever." An alarming photograph of two kids looking no older than nine, lighting up joints, accompanies the article. "Pot smoking and dealing have moved down through the school grades and age levels and have become an integral part of the experience of growing up," declares an article in the *New York Times Magazine.*[8]

School personnel began making similar observations in the late seventies. "Several years ago high school students were experiment-ing. Now we are finding people coming into high school who have started using drugs in fourth, fifth, or sixth grade and who get into a heavy dependence by junior high school," says the dean of students at a Connecticut high school. Even teenagers themselves began to comment on the change, often with a certain indignation. "I started smoking pot in tenth grade, when I went to boarding school," remi-nisces a college student. "At that time pot hadn't started filtering down to the lower grades yet. It was still a pretty much high school thing to do. But now little *kids* are turning on!"

And yet a decline in supervision is not the entire story. Even in the fifties there were undersupervised children, whose parents were divorced or whose mothers worked, but who nevertheless did not become pregnant at thirteen or even "go all the way" and who did not smoke anything stronger than an occasional Camel or Lucky Strike. The difference is that sex was still in the closet, in those days before X-rated movies and *The Joy of Sex,* and drugs were unavailable outside the lower reaches of society. It took a combination of un-supervised children *and* a permissive, highly charged sexual atmo-sphere *and* an influx of easily acquired drugs *and* the wherewithal to buy them to bring about precocious experimentation by younger and younger children. This occurred in the mid-seventies.

The wherewithal to buy drugs: this raises a frequently asked ques-tion. If parents are concerned that their children are buying drugs, why not simply cut off their allowances and achieve control in that simple way? Parents who have tried that strategy attest to its failure. "The kids have all the bargaining chips," a New York father of two teenage daughters explains. "When we told Linda that we were going to cut off her allowance because she was buying marijuana, she looked us coolly in the eye and said, 'OK, then I'll have to deal [sell drugs to others].' Needless to say, we didn't cut off her allowance." Other children whose parents do stop providing them with spending money turn to baby-sitting for funds, or get short-term jobs after school in ice-cream stores or the like. Or they become drug dealers, hugely escalating the dangers that their drug involvement presents.

As a divorced New York mother, whose thirteen-year-old son was suspended from school after being caught smoking marijuana with a group of classmates, concludes: "I don't think any parent today can really stop a sixth- or seventh-grader from smoking pot or getting into sex. The pot is so available, the kids have the money, and they have so much freedom, so little supervision, what with all of us having to work just to survive. Perhaps if we had done something different during all those years they were little, maybe we'd have more control today, maybe they'd just do what we tell them. Maybe some brand-new parent today who decides 'My baby is not going to smoke pot at twelve' will figure out some child-rearing method to help achieve that, some kind of fear tactics, or strictness. But given the way we parents have raised our children, I just don't think there's any way to control these kids once they reach puberty."

EARLY EMANCIPATION

Consider the dilemma of the following far from untypical New York family—mother, father, and two children raised in a free, easygoing manner.

When the children are still babies the parents acquire a place in the country where the family may repair for weekends and longer vacations. There the parents introduce the growing youngsters to birds and flowers and the beauties of nature. They watch ants building anthills. They feed the ducks and geese. They plant a garden, start a compost heap. The parents both have jobs and love the change of pace that weekends in the country provide. They enjoy the feeling of being a family that comes over them when they all settle down in their country house. They don't even have a television set there, though the children "unfortunately watch much too much television during the week," in the mother's words.

The years pass—not all that many years, either. The children are now eleven and twelve, in the sixth and seventh grades. And while the parents' love of their country place has not diminished—on the contrary, it has become a passionate attachment by now—the children are getting restless. The wonders of nature leave them cold, suddenly, and they pass the chill along. The rabbits and ducks and muskrats and scrapbooks of pressed leaves—all that is baby stuff. There seems to be nothing to do in the country. They miss their TV programs. Mainly, they have acquired a group of friends with whom they have formed *their* passionate attachment. Suddenly they don't want to go to the country with their parents every Friday evening. The weekends for them are filled with more attractive alternatives: Mary's having a birthday party; Bobby's invited me to go to the movies with him. Even schoolwork is invoked as an excuse: "We have to write a paper for history class."

The parents are suddenly faced with a real dilemma, or rather, a *tri*lemma: they can force the kids to come with them to the country; they can stay home in the city with the kids; or they can go to the country and leave the kids behind. The first alternative—the forced march to the country—proves to be intolerable. The kids become hateful. They act conspicuously bored, sullen, hangdog about helping in the smallest way, rude, ungrateful for all their parents' efforts to keep them amused. Moreover, under these circumstances the children's resistance to the country rapidly develops into a blind hatred for nature and all things not made by man. The parents' simple pleasures in country life are poisoned. Their old feeling of cozy family solidarity seems a travesty.

The second alternative, to stay at home and give up their weekends to keep an eye on the kids? Why, who will water the garden? What about their own lives? It seems a terrible sacrifice.

To leave the children behind, unsupervised? It's unthinkable! They are only children! Do they have the judgment, at eleven and twelve, to be left by themselves? What about all those horror stories about kids getting involved with drugs and sex these days? And yet the children *act* so old, so knowing; there hardly seems a trace of childishness about them. The parents can no longer use child psychology on them to get them to behave in certain ways and not in others. Somehow, the kids seem to be pretty much on their own already . . .

At first some compromises are worked out: We'll stay home one weekend, and you kids come with us to the country the next weekend. But this doesn't work for long. The weekends in the country with the unwilling kids are unbearable; the weekends when they are all together in the city are difficult.

Finally, the unthinkable becomes a reality: the parents go, the kids stay. Unsupervised. Or invited to spend the weekend at a friend's house. Trusted until proved untrustworthy, which happens not infrequently when a neighbor reports, several months later, that the kids are having parties. When the parents discover that there are drugs involved. When the child with whom the kids are supposed to be staying also turns out to have parents who go away for weekends.

Children of past generations had to emancipate themselves from their families too at some point, to pursue interests of their own, friends of their own. But the breakaway point was considerably later, and that's the great difference. Today's parents remember rebelling when they were fifteen or sixteen. But today's children are often out of control before they reach puberty.

Among the most poignant stories are those of parents who have struggled to preserve a close, intact family, who have tried to maintain protective standards in their child rearing, who have taken great pains to supervise their children far beyond the current norm, and who have nevertheless lost control. Yet often it is the very discrepancy between these parents' careful standards and the greater freedom their children's friends enjoy that has created the problem.

"It's not that we just abandoned our kids and let them do anything they wanted," reports the father of two teenage daughters who experimented with LSD along with classmates at their progressive New York school. "But no matter how careful we were to always be home when the kids had parties, and how many weekends we stayed home instead of going to the country just so that the kids wouldn't be unsupervised, still there were always those 'teenage

Cubas' for them to get together in—islands of freedom where they could do anything they wanted. These, of course, were the homes of kids whose parents weren't as careful as we were—sometimes single parents who were busy with their own social lives, or simply very casual or very fatalistic folks who truly had given up on trying to protect their kids. Short of forbidding our kids ever to leave the house, or checking on their friends in a police-state kind of way, there was nothing much we could do."

A MODERN FAMILY SAGA

"The bottom line is that no matter how you do it, it's going to be a hard job being a parent and it's going to be a hard job being a kid nowadays."

Dorothy Green and her husband Bill are an example of parents who have brought up their children in a different style than their own parents. "The old way," Dorothy Green continues, "the parents did their job, they provided for you, but they didn't expect to be friends with their kids. They expected respect. We expect much more of the relationship with our children. We're franker with them about our own lives, about our own problems, even our marital problems. I never discussed anything at all with my parents."

The Greens' family problems began when their younger daughter Betsy was thirteen. For almost three years they watched helplessly as their relationship with their daughter deteriorated and her life went in dangerous directions. Dorothy Green tells some of the details:

"Betsy was thirteen, I guess, the summer she began to smoke dope with us. We always smoked openly at home, but we never let Betsy or her friends smoke at our house. We didn't think it would be fair to the other parents. But that summer we smoked a lot, and she'd be there sitting with us, and we knew that she had already smoked with her friends already—all her friends started in seventh grade—and so we just included her when we turned on.

"We felt closer to her that summer than we ever had. Her sister was away for the first time, and it was a great opportunity for her to have us to herself. She was still a child, really, but everything was so relaxed in the country.

"I don't know when Betsy first started smoking dope. It was certainly long before that summer. She traveled with a pack of girls from school. They all looked alike, had long hair, wore tattered blue jeans, and they had to do everything together. This started in sixth grade, and I know that by eighth grade they were all smoking a lot of dope. In retrospect I think we probably should have been much stricter about it. But we were feeling, 'Well, this is what we do, and why pretend? She knows we smoke.'

"In eighth grade I began to be worried about the lack of motivation in her life. She and her friends never did anything. They never seemed interested in anything, motivated by anything—except rock. That they'd discuss endlessly. In eighth grade all her friends were going to *Rocky Horror,* * and we said that she couldn't go to a movie that started at midnight—that was too late. Well, it turned out that she went anyway, when she was spending the weekend at a friend's house.

"In ninth grade she got caught smoking in school. She had told me that none of them took dope during school hours, but she hadn't told the truth. She was suspended, and the school made a big fuss. That was good! They ought to make a fuss. That makes things easier for the parents!

"Around tenth grade Betsy stopped wanting to go with us to the country for weekends. She wanted to be with her friends, and this seemed perfectly normal to us. She seemed old enough to take care of herself for a weekend. But one day in the spring we got a call from a mother asking whether we knew that the kids were having parties at our apartment while we were away for weekends. Well, we hadn't known.

"A party nowadays is not an occasion when you send out invitations, like in our day. It's where the gang is meeting that night. Well, this gang was using the apartment for all-night parties, involving drugs and sex, with some older guys who had graduated high school but hadn't gone to college. Betsy and we had a terrible confrontation

*_The Rocky Horror Show,_ a cult movie about transvestites.

about her having parties, about her lying to us that she wasn't going to do that.

"I got in touch with the parents of all the other girls and tried to get them to establish the same rules about when the girls had to be home. All the parents agreed that the girls were being horrible to them. And we were still in a state of shock about Betsy's behavior. Here was this child who had never been unpleasant except to her sister, and suddenly she had turned into a monster. Just the classic case, the way people tell you about teenagers. She was so rude, so nasty, so oblivious to our feelings.

"She wouldn't tell us the phone numbers of where she was going. She wouldn't come home until all hours, and one night didn't come home at all. One night we tried not letting her out of the house— physically barring the door. That was very tough. She constantly provoked us, and I think she *wanted* us to do something. One time I hit her, I actually slapped her face, she was being so unbelievably provocative. I think she immediately realized that she deserved it. It was as if she and her friends were possessed by something, as if she wasn't entirely rational and didn't know why she was doing all this.

"They used marijuana and they had coke, and sex, of course. And I know they took LSD sometimes. They were using this apartment near Columbia that a group of boys had rented as a sort of crash pad. Finally we found out where it was and got the phone number, and then we and the other parents of the girls began harassing them— calling at three in the morning. We just wanted our kids home.

"But I think the guys began to get sick of it and realized that this would happen when they got involved with girls that young. All this time we kept blaming the boys: they had led these innocent girls astray. But really, that wasn't the way it had happened. The girls were initiating the trouble. They were all sort of hysterical. I kept thinking of *The Crucible*. We tended to blame everything but her. We overblamed the boys, and her friends, because we didn't want to believe that our own kid could be so nasty. That's why the *Exorcist* syndrome, the notion of being possessed, is so enticing. We kept storming up there, making scenes, until I think the guys ended the relationship.

"There we were, put in the role of old-fashioned, repressive parents. That's what was so bizarre. Because we're just the opposite, really. But somehow Betsy had to create us in that image, had to make us into oppressive parents. I kept saying, 'I'm being put in a role and I don't want to play it! I hate this role!' But I *had* to take on that role.

"Finally we all went to a family therapist. It took some persuading to get Betsy to come, but I think she was ready for a truce and that's why she finally agreed. We went about eight sessions, and it was really very helpful. Betsy was ready for a change. She was worn out. It's hard to tell what the therapist did that made us all change. But among other things, she told my husband and me to stop smoking dope. And we did."

CAUTIONARY TALES

In the days before childhood came to be seen as a special, golden age, before children were differentiated from adults in hundreds of great and little ways, parents did not hesitate to try to control their children's behavior by means of cautionary tales or poems, writings that emphasized the frightening realities of life and the terrifying uncertainties of death and the afterlife.

A contemporary historian, John Demos, has written about such a cautionary passage in a diary of Cotton Mather in which the Puritan minister describes to his four-year-old daughter, in graphic terms, the details of his own impending death: "I took my little daughter Katy into my study and then told my child I am to die shortly and she must, when I am dead, remember everything I now said unto her. I set before her the sinful condition of her nature. . . ."[9] Demos comments: "The calculated appeal to fear affronts our sense of the needs and sensibilities of childhood," thus implying that a more protective attitude prevails today. But Demos was writing in a bygone era, though it was only ten years ago. From the time the new view of childhood as a time of preparation began to penetrate deeply into the American consciousness, parents have had to adjust to the knowledge that they are no longer in control of many dangerous and difficult aspects of their children's lives. Recognizing that they cannot any longer protect their children from life-threatening experimentation with drugs or alcohol, or keep them from blighting their future through sexual irresponsibility, they have come to adopt some of those old strategies used by parents of the past.

Today's desperate parents frequently hasten their children's fall from innocence in the hope that sordid and frightening information may impel their children to exercise that most adult of virtues, self-control. A mother whose twelve-year-old son was suspended from school after being caught smoking marijuana in the boys' bathroom, in a desperate effort to persuade the lad to stay away from illegal drugs decided to give him a vivid description of what might face him if he were arrested and taken to a juvenile detention center: "I told Philip graphically what might happen to a boy like him if he had to spend the night at Spofford or some other juvenile-offenders. I told him he'd possibly have his eyes gouged out. And he'd certainly be raped by other boys, because he's young and pretty and white. I think he believed me."

Ironically, the very medium so instrumental in making parents feel out of control—television—is frequently used to try to keep children in hand. Many parents encourage their pre-teenage children to watch frightening and sexually explicit television documentaries in the hope that these will serve as cautionary tales to prevent the behavior parents feel incapable of controlling.

A sixth-grade girl reports: "My parents wanted me to watch this program, *Diary of a Teenage Hitchhiker*. I hadn't even wanted to watch it, but they thought I should see it. There was this one girl in it who beat up a guy who was about to rape her. And then there was this other girl who knew there's a danger of getting raped when you hitchhike but she did it anyway, and she got all beat up and had to go to the hospital. When the movie was over my mom said, 'See, you'd better not ever hitchhike.' And then she said, 'When you start going out on dates you better be careful who you go out with.' Actually," the child added thoughtfully, "that movie wasn't rated R. It was PG because they didn't actually show you the girl getting raped—they just showed you the car pulling off to the side of the road and then her T-shirt being torn off. Because I guess they wanted kids my age to see it and learn about things."

Another sixth-grader told of a "scary" program about child pornography that her parents encouraged her to watch. "The point of the movie," she declared, "was to show kids what not to do, like not to get involved with a guy like that one, who did things to the little girl. If kids watch this program they'll be prepared for things like that happening to them."

After School Specials, a highly recommended series screened on schooldays at 4:30 P.M. and aimed at school-age children, frequently chooses subjects of a cautionary nature for its young audience. A typical program was "Stoned," which, as a review described it, "takes a representative marijuana story and tells it with the lean determination of a morality tale." A fifth-grader recently recounted her version of another of these, in a paradoxically childish, lisping voice: "I saw this *After School Special* about how these teenagers get involved with boys. Then this girl *really* gets involved with a boy, you know, they have intercourse, and then she has a baby and she doesn't know what to do with it, and the boy hitchhikes away, and she can't control the baby, it just cries all the time, and so she starts to take drugs, and then she doesn't realize she's expecting another baby, and the baby she already has has multiple sclerosis, so she leaves the baby in a backpack on a bridge and she jumps off and kills herself." She sighs slightly as she concludes her earnest retelling of what may be the most astonishing collection of warnings all rolled into one: against teenage sex, lack of contraception, drugs, abortion, permissive child rearing ("she can't control the baby"), and perhaps even multiple sclerosis.

Some parents are selectively cautionary in their child rearing. A parent who protectively withholds certain adult information from her two children, aged eight and eleven—about money problems, for instance ("We're really feeling the pinch once again, but I don't think that's an anxiety children ought to share")—says, "If I hear about any drug-related problem, no matter how horrible, I'll immediately tell the children about it. Because I want them to be really scared of drugs. I think drugs are terrifying, and I don't want my kids involved with them. I show them factual material from the newspapers, or TV documentaries."

Even the youngest children today are not spared a cautionary warning against feared dangers. An article in the *Washington Post* of September 13, 1980, describing a lurid antidrug play, *The Death of*

O. D. Walker, put on by teenagers in Washington, D.C., and sponsored by a public agency for the purpose of "bringing home to children the serious and sometimes tragic consequences of drug abuse," is illustrated by a photograph showing a row of very young children, three-to-five-year-olds, watching the grim play with wide eyes and open mouths.

Telling cautionary tales may help to keep children from taking foolish risks and may indeed prepare them for dangers that lie ahead; nevertheless, this strategy has a depressing effect on children's outlook towards their own future. Whereas children once looked forward with impatience to growing up, many of them today have a cautious if not out-and-out fearful attitude about what lies ahead. Without the perspective of maturity, they distort the horror stories they see on television and in the movies, applying them to their own life, and they begin to feel out of control of their future. They lose some of the optimism and hopefulness that once seemed a natural part of childhood.

An eleven-year-old girl says: "Sometimes I think, 'Ugh, I don't ever want to grow up and be a teenager.' It's like when I hear about drugs and pot and stuff and I'm afraid I might get into it. Right now I really think it's bad for you, but later on everybody might be doing it so I might try it and then get addicted. I'm really scared about that."

Another sixth-grader admits: "It's kind of scary to think about getting older because I once saw this movie about alcoholics. And there was this teenage girl and she didn't want to take a drink and her boyfriend said 'What's the matter, are you chicken?' and she says 'No, no!' and takes a drink and becomes an alcoholic. And then at the end you see her drunk and boys are pouring beer down her throat and she gets in a car accident and three people die on her account. Finally she joins Alcoholics Anonymous, but her life is ruined."

GALLOWS HUMOR

Some parents who feel out of control choose not to frighten their children with lurid tales. Rather, they indulge in a form of gallows humor, deliberately kidding about their specific fears, hoping against hope that this may somehow, perhaps magically, turn a dangerous situation into a mere joke. A fourteen-year-old girl described such a parental strategy: "When I went to see *Fantasia* my father began joking around and said, 'Now don't get stoned or anything!' I'm pretty sure my father is against drugs—he doesn't know that I've smoked marijuana—but he sort of jokes about it anyway."

The fact that this girl was not altogether certain that her father's joking comments indicated disapprobation and anxiety (which a subsequent interview with the father revealed to be the case) suggests that the gallows-humor strategy is not particularly effective as a deterrent. Indeed, a mother describing her son's serious problems with marijuana recalls saying to him in a joking way, "Don't get caught smoking dope, you guys!" when her thirteen-year-old son started going to rock concerts with a group of friends. Today she thinks back and wonders if the impact of these warnings might have been unfortunate. "I sometimes wonder whether he didn't take those jokes as a sort of green light from me to begin smoking," she admits thoughtfully, adding, "He probably sensed some of my ambivalence. There's a part of me that wants my kid to be with it, to be hip, and accepted by the other kids. By joking about it I think I was sending him mixed messages."

PARENTAL FATALISM

In the face of tales of widespread child precocity, great numbers of parents, after watching the tenth documentary on junior potheads and reading yet another story about child prostitution, child alcoholism, child pornography, child sex orgies, and the like, develop a fatalistic attitude towards the dangers that threaten their children in today's society. In his novel *Something Happened*, Joseph Heller paints a well-observed portrait of such a parent, musing about his young-teenage daughter:

It is too late, I feel, for me to save her, or even to help her, and I really don't think I would know what to do anymore to try (except to sit apathetically and watch her go her unhappy way). It would do no more good for me to try to change her now than it has done in the past, when she was more credulous and suggestible, and more eager to please. I have tried; I have taunted, reasoned, thundered, whined, disciplined, flattered and cajoled, to no avail and perhaps much harm, until I confessed to myself one day that it was not merely hypocritical of me, but futile, and therefore foolish. Then I stopped. . . . I know I have no power over her now. If I knew she were about to become a heroin addict and then a common prostitute, I wouldn't know what to do to avert it. I would rail and curse *my* fate; but none of that would help. So I wouldn't try at all.[10]

Heller captures well the fatalism of the modern parent who has gone through the various stages of fear, panic, frantic effort to *do* something, resignation, and finally acceptance, not unlike the stages a terminally ill patient passes through in preparation for death. Most parents today, it appears, pass through similar stages as they make a mental adjustment to the fact that much of their children's childhood will be out of their control.

Once acceptance has set in, many parents hardly recall their former anxiety. "Drugs haven't really been a problem with our kids," the suburban father of three children aged fourteen, twelve, and eleven asserts to an interviewer. "Daniel, the fourteen-year-old, has played around with grass starting around middle school, seventh and eighth grade, and I suspect that at least one of the girls has experimented with pot, she practically said it. But we feel it's absolutely inevitable these days. They seem to be doing OK."

Some parental fatalism is encouraged by the more worldly and unchildlike image children present today, giving them the appearance of being more grown up. "When I first heard about smoking pot in junior high school I was absolutely horrified," a divorced mother raising two daughters tells. "And when Kathy was six years old, say, I would have just died to think of her taking drugs at thirteen. But now that she's actually thirteen I can see that she's pretty grown up. She's sophisticated and intelligent enough, I feel, to know when to be careful. And so when she asked me what I think about her smoking pot, I told her I don't object as long as she doesn't become a pothead. After all, it's all right for everybody else in the world to escape reality once in a while—why not for a kid?"

There are times when parents' fatalistic acceptance of their children's involvement with drugs is tinged with a peculiar sort of encouragement that the children do not fail to sense. It goes like this: The parents really don't *want* their twelve-year-old to smoke dope. But if the kid is *going to do it anyhow,* if everyone else does it (as *Time* and *Newsweek* and *CBS Reports* would have them believe), then perhaps there is something wrong with trying to have their child *not* do it and be different. The experts can write themselves blue in the face about the adverse effects of cannabis on young adolescents, and yet parents who try to buck the tide can't help but feel like fossils. Besides, an irrational yet common feeling makes them wonder: If everybody is doing it, can it really be so bad? Maybe the experts are wrong.

Parents' acceptance of their loss of control is sometimes even accompanied by a feeling of liberation. As a New York father put it: "There's an up side to that feeling of being out of control. It's not altogether a matter of everyone throwing up their arms and crying, 'I don't know what to do about this!' The other side is that feeling of not being responsible any longer. 'It's not my problem,' I can think. 'It's *their* problem.' "

The experts themselves offer little guidance to the helpless parent; often these advisers only feed parental fatalism by adding their own. In an unequivocally negative article about the effects on children of smoking marijuana, after citing evidence that it causes chromosome damage, decreases the sperm count, atrophies brain cells, lowers motivation in school, and turns good students into failures, the author offers no concrete plan for action. Instead, he writes:

> We know it is futile to barge onto the scene like the cops, mad and
> frustrated. What we can do is change the climate in which mari-

juana and other drugs are used. We do this by updating our drug information and learning the facts, especially the gross, unavoidable facts of what we see in our own children and students. We must also, without withdrawing our affection and support, confront adolescents with their own destructive defenses; and we must by all means stop reinforcing those defenses by becoming dramatically afraid or pious about the whole business.[11]

That's it for advice, apart from a suggestion that parents not be "too timid or too preoccupied to sit down with their children for the purposes of discussing drugs and establishing rules governing their use." That's it? But what should parents do if the kids break those rules? Is it enough not to be timid or pious? With their children's brain cells possibly atrophying, their sperm count dropping, their genetic future slipping down the drain along with their marks in school, do parents solve anything by "learning the facts"? Small wonder that parents are fatalistic. Even the experts know there's nothing much that can be done.

In light of this fatalism, most of the organizations that deal with children's drug use direct their efforts towards *the parents' mental health* rather than towards controlling the children's undesirable activities. The major thrust of Families Anonymous, an organization patterned after Alcoholics Anonymous for parents of drug-taking children, is to help the parents accept their essential powerlessness. The first of the twelve precepts of the Families Anonymous credo reads: "We admitted that we were powerless over drugs and other people's lives—that *our* lives had become unmanageable." Another exhorts parents to resolve "not to *do* things for the person I am trying to help, but to *be* things; not to try to control and change his actions, but through understanding, to change *my* reactions."[12]

And so parents direct their efforts towards their own survival rather than their children's. Just as parents of the distant past were forced to accept the fact that their children's chances for surviving infancy were small, and were obliged to accept the necessity of child labor, child exploitation, child suffering and neglect, so today's parents are forced to recognize that after a certain brief number of years they must lose control of their children's lives.

LOOKING FOR A SAFE HAVEN

A small number of parents continue to fight current trends towards precocity by looking for ways to perpetuate a protective childhood for their children. A mother of an eleven-year-old girl, distressed by a recent meeting for parents of fifth-graders at her daughter's progressive New York private school, gives this report:

"The meeting started out with one mother getting up and saying, 'My daughter is totally preoccupied with sex. She acts like she's sixteen, is only interested in clothes and her looks, and treats us as if we were loathsome insects.' Well, everybody laughed, but then the majority of parents spoke up and admitted that their children seemed to be getting out of control and they didn't know how to handle it. Parent after parent complained about their children's precocious behavior, rudeness, and rebelliousness.

"Well, it hasn't struck Emily yet. She's still a little girl, thank goodness. But I think it's kind of a contagious thing kids pick up from their peers. So I have definitely decided to take her out of that school after the summer and put her in a more protected environment. I just don't want to take the chance. I've found a very old-fashioned school in our neighborhood. It's semireligious, but the program is strictly academic. I'm hoping the other families there will be more like mine, more traditional, somehow."

The admissions director of a Jewish parochial school in New York confirms that in recent years there has been a significant increase in applications from nonreligious parents who admittedly choose the school in the hope that the religious environment will protect their children from some of the dangers that threaten them today. Other parents, she reports, feel there is a chance that their children will not undergo the dreaded personality change—the "teenage-werewolf" syndrome—if they spend their school years in a strict religious institution.

For similar reasons some parents choose to send their sons and daughters to one-sex schools. They hope this may retard some of the social and sexual precocity that they observe in other children and would like to forestall in their own.* A mother who sent two sons to one of the few remaining all-boys' private schools in New York confesses: "I went to a coed school myself, and I really *believe* in coeducation. But I decided to send my sons to a rather old-fashioned boys' school because I hoped that some of the wild things that go on at other schools, the drugs and sex and all that, might not be as likely to happen there. And I think I was right. My boys grew up a little socially retarded, and I feel a little guilty that they didn't have quite as much fun as I had in high school. But they did well in school, they developed some great interests, made some great friends, and didn't get into the sort of trouble a lot of my friends' kids seemed to fall into. And believe me, they're making up for the social lacks in college! They're having a ball!"

OUT-OF-CONTROL TELEVISION

Even the most old-fashioned, protection-minded parents today recognize that no matter how cleverly they plan their children's lives, how cloisterlike a school they choose, how carefully they hide their own troubles, how self-sacrificingly they conduct their lives, nevertheless they have little chance of controlling their children's exposure to every variety of adult sexuality, every permutation and combination of human brutality and violence, every aspect of sickness, disease, and suffering, every frightening possibility for natural and man-made disaster that might impinge on an innocent and carefree childhood. There is always the television set waiting to undo all their careful plans. Even that tiny percentage of eccentrics, far less than one percent of the American population, who choose to live without television in their homes cannot hope to sanitize their children from

---

*It is not insignificant that since the social and sexual revolution of the sixties most one-sex schools, once a common phenomenon, have become coed.

its impact altogether. Often programs that careful parents consider unsuitable are screened for children during school hours—for social studies classes, for instance. And while diehard parents can try to enjoy a wholesome, old-fashioned family life without television's magnetic pull, there is still a set (or two or three) in the homes of most of their children's friends.

Without a doubt television's presence in the home has contributed to the out-of-control feeling so pervasive among parents today. Of course, parents of the past were never in complete control of their children's media consumption either, be it the books they read or the radio programs they listened to. But the material available to children today on television, particularly on cable TV, and to a lesser degree in books and magazines is far less appropriate for their consumption than what they were likely to run into in their reading, viewing, or listening in the past.

A New York mother reports: "Once when I was out late my thirteen-year-old and nine-year-old stayed up and watched *Midnight Blue* on cable TV [a sexually explicit program aired at midnight in many communities around America]. The next day they made a big point of telling me exactly what they saw on the show, some 'gross' product they showed that was used to masturbate with. The very thought of me telling *my* mother about such a thing—she would have died! Of course, in my youth you simply wouldn't have found such a program on television." The mother, a divorced single parent, adds somewhat defensively, "I just can't stay home and guard them every minute. I have my own life to lead," once again confirming the connection between decreased supervision and precocious experience.

A New York father tells of his ten-year-old son: "In the fall we couldn't understand why all my son's friends kept coming over on Friday to spend the night. We almost always go out on Fridays, but that seemed fine. We couldn't imagine the kids wouldn't be OK on their own. Well, we finally found out that they were all watching this pornographic show on cable TV. We watched it ourselves and we were horrified. Even our son admitted that he thought it was pretty disgusting. But they all wanted to watch it. We told him not to turn it on in the future, and I think we talked him out of it, although we don't check every Friday—nor do we cancel dinner invitations or parties because of it, I'm afraid."

Children themselves confirm to an interviewer that their parents can't control what they watch on television or in the movies (often movies on cable TV). "My mother doesn't know," said a childish-looking ten-year-old girl, "but my younger sister and I watched *Pretty Baby, Ten, The Exorcist,* and *Lipstick* [all movies rated R] on *Home Box Office.*"

"My mom would be shocked to know what I know," an eleven-year-old boy cheerfully admitted. "I wouldn't want her to think I'm perverted or something, so I'm glad she doesn't know the things I watch."

"My parents won't let me watch *HBO,*" a twelve-year-old from a stable, protective family informed an interviewer, "but I watch at my friend's house all the time."

I T ' S   N O T   W H A T   T H E Y   W A T C H

Of course television *is* deeply implicated in the changed image of today's child, and of course television *has* played a crucial role in hastening the end of that protected stage of life that was once known as childhood. But not necessarily in the way most people think. To consider that television's effect on children's lives is primarily a function of its content—of the programs that children watch—is to ignore the medium's real impact. To believe that a nation of eight- or nine- or ten-year-olds could have lost their definition as children and achieved a new integration into adult life mainly as a result of watching *General Hospital* or *Dallas* or sexy commercials or even *Midnight Blue* is to see but the thin top layer of a powerful agent of change.

To be sure, the programs children watch make a difference too. Through television they gain entry into a confusing adult world that cannot help but shake their confidence and trust in those elders who once seemed so omniscient, powerful, and good. But their trust is not diminished all that much—at least not by television itself. Child experts agree that even scary or sexual programs do not deeply affect children who grow up in normal, reasonably happy families. It is when other things go haywire in a child's life—when his parents divorce, for instance—that television's actual images may have a deeper and more negative influence.

True, television programs teach children sophisticated words and phrases and cause them to imitate unchildlike ways of moving, gesturing, dancing, and behaving that create an illusion of maturity not necessarily based on any emotional reality. This too is a factor in childhood's change, but a somewhat superficial one. If a child were to be raised in the way parents reared children in the pretelevision era, it is likely that no amount of sexy imitations he or she might learn, verbal or gestural, would obscure the fact that this was a child imitating a TV program.

But television's very presence in the home has worked to alter children's lives in ways that have nothing to do with *what* they might be watching. Parents' use of the medium as a child-rearing aid is one such way. Its easy availability as a child amuser, baby-sitter, and problem solver has altered long-established child-rearing patterns, allowing parents to coexist with their children without establishing those rules and limitations that parents once had to impose on children simply for survival's sake. Before television, parents had to make sure that their kids could be relied upon to "mind" when necessary, not to interrupt adult conversation, not to demand attention when the parent was busy or instant gratification of their every wish; otherwise nothing would ever get done around the house, and the parents would go crazy. It was crucial for parents who had to live in close proximity with children, to eat with them at the same table, to sit with them in the same living room, that the children learn early how to behave in acceptable, disciplined ways. Television, however, provided an easy alternative to parental discipline. Instead of having to establish rules and limits, an arduous and often frustrating job, instead of having to work at socializing children in order to make them more agreeable to live with, parents could solve all these problems by resorting to the television set. "Go watch TV" were the magic words. Now mothers could cook dinner in peace, or prepare their briefs for the next day's case, or whatever. No need to work on training the children to play quietly while mothers and fathers discussed a family matter without interruption.

Television brought peace—but at a price. Without establishing firm rules and precise boundaries, parents never defined for the children precisely what the roles of the adults and the children in the family were to be. And without having to take an authoritative position right from the start, parents never gained the control of their children that their counterparts of the past achieved quite inevitably, out of sheer necessity. A new equality between adults and children became possible.[13]

THE NEW EQUALITY

EARLY DECISION MAKING

In the not-so-long-ago past, during that lengthy period between infancy and adolescence known as childhood, one of the well-known characteristics of "real" children was a relatively docile acceptance of their role as dependent beings who didn't have many choices about their lives or even their daily behavior.

Of course, American children have always been less dependent, more "equal," somehow, than their European counterparts, as European observers from De Toqueville on have noted for at least two centuries. But the greater independence and assertiveness of American children when compared with European children simply attests to the compromise American parents have always made between their desire to protect and their need to encourage self-reliance. In reality, it was often a bit of an act "for the children's sake," encouraging them to learn to make decisions and giving them choices rather than being authoritarian and undemocratic and telling them what to do. Though somewhat indirectly, parents of the past generally operated with authority and confidence and kept a firm hold on the reins at least until the child reached his middle teens and began to forcibly wrest them from his parents' hands. And in spite of a certain permissive streak that has characterized American child rearing from pioneer days, the broad picture was, until recently, one of strictly defined roles that were maintained by both adults and children.

This is not to say that children in times past always behaved in the way they were supposed to—quite the contrary: part of their definition as children was to try to "get away with it," to misbehave, to break the rules. But a structure of rules existed that they came to understand well and that gave them a certain protection.

An example of this paradoxical connection between children's misbehavior of the past and their secure definition as children may be seen in Booth Tarkington's *Penrod*, a once popular and still psychologically valid portrait of a fictional boy in the throes of childhood, whose pranks and misbehavior were enjoyed by all generations from 1914, when the book was published, until recent years. In one episode, a wretched Penrod, disgusted by his assigned role in the Sunday school play, uses all his boyish wiles to sabotage the event. But never would he have dreamed of open rebellion, of saying, "No, I refuse to play the Child Launcelot. It's a ridiculous role, degrading to children," as a child today might easily declare, a child who has grown used to having a say about the choices in his life from an early age. Rather, Penrod accepts it as completely inevitable that he has to do what is required of him by the adults in charge of his life. Choice was virtually absent for a child raised in that old child-rearing style. Children did not need to involve themselves in making the meaningful or even the insignificant decisions in their lives, because adults— it appears to us as we look back—had an abiding confidence that they were capable of making the right choices for children themselves.

Is there any way to demonstrate that children really *are* forced to make more decisions today, as seems to be the case, or might this be an example of a change that only *appears* to have happened, as each set of parents observes the next generation coming along and feels that everything is somehow different?

One source of information about changes in children's decision making may be found among salesmen who have worked for many years in stores that handle children's goods. From their unique vantage point these old-timers can assess changes in parents' and children's behavior over the years. Many such informants declare that children today are indeed taking a far greater part in decisions about what clothes or what shoes to buy, and at much younger ages, than children in the past. A salesman at an established children's shoe store on the Upper West Side in New York speaks emphatically of the change: "Kids are dictating more to Mama what kind of shoes or sneakers they want," he asserts. "We see women come in with a

two-year-old child who say, 'The child must like the shoes, otherwise
he won't wear them.' In the past—ten years ago, for instance—this
didn't happen, not with children that young. And the older kids
completely dictate to their parents what they want to wear. If there's
a dispute, the kids win."

The shoe salesman explains children's new assertiveness: "The
mother wants to teach the child to know its own mind. So the parents
are encouraging children to make decisions. That's why parents
today are giving the child more what *he* wants than what the mother
would like to have on the child's foot."

As it happens, as the salesman is being interviewed, another salesman nearby is dealing with a mother and her three-year-old child
who provide an example of the very change being investigated. "No,
I don't want that shoe!" the child says emphatically (loud enough to
have the words immortalized on the interviewer's tape recording).
"Well, dear, which shoe *do* you want?" the mother asks helplessly.
"Just tell us which shoe you want. You don't *have* to have a shoe you
don't like."

NO MORE HEROES

One of the greatest differences between adults and children was long
considered to be that children are helpless and dependent while
adults are powerful and independent. It was upon this confident
belief that adults based much of the authority they exercised over
children. We may safely say that the distance between children and
adults in regard to their relative authority and control has significantly diminished within the last two decades. Why has this change
occurred at this particular time?

A major blow to adult authority in the eyes of children was dealt
by those political and social events of the last fifteen or so years that
caused a public erosion of confidence in the benevolence of the
elected government. The growing mistrust of elected officials that
began to gain momentum in America during the Vietnam War and
reached its apogee during the Watergate crisis filtered down into the
child's world via newspapers and television news. As children became aware that adults are not always honorable, that they use bad

language (as the very President of the United States, a man sharing the same office with such mythological heroes as George Washington and Thomas Jefferson, was shown to do in the Watergate transcripts), that they lie, cheat, and behave in fact much the way children know that they themselves are inclined to behave unless restrained by adult rules, their attitude towards the adult world, and specifically towards their own parents, undergoes subtle changes in the direction of suspicion and disrespect.

But rather than their direct effect on children's attitudes, the impact of events such as Watergate and Abscam on adults themselves brought about the most significant changes in adult-child relations. Adults were, if anything, far more severely shaken by the seemingly endless series of disillusionment with authority figures than children could have been—children, after all, have fewer illusions in the first place. As adults felt themselves betrayed by their faithless leaders (who had, in a sense, stood *in loco parentis* to them as governments always do to their citizens), their ability to act with authority, certainty, and confidence towards their own children was weakened. A New York mother who grew up in the simpler times of the 1940s and 1950s describes an event that made her come to understand how a changed attitude towards authority has affected her life as a parent:

"I was trying to understand why my childhood seemed so simple, while my children are having such a rocky time. A lot of things seem pretty much the same for them as they were for me when I was growing up. My husband and I have a good marriage, we have a close family, we're pretty well off, but not enough to spoil the kids. Then the other day I happened to pull out of my bookcase an old copy of *Alice in Wonderland* my father had given me when I was in the hospital having my tonsils out. As I opened the book I noticed an inscription in my father's handwriting, dated April 12, 1945. I would have been ten years old then. 'This book was bought a few hours before our great President Franklin Delano Roosevelt died.' As I read those words I had the strangest feeling. The idea that my father would have written those words 'our great President' just amazed me. It seemed so childlike to have that sort of feeling about a politician, almost like believing in Santa Claus. Nobody feels that way about presidents nowadays.

"Of course, the sort of feeling my father had about Roosevelt was precisely the sort of feeling we children had about our parents when we were growing up. We felt that they were above us, that they knew what they were doing and were out for our good, and that they would always *make everything all right.* I know my own two kids don't have that sort of feeling about us as parents, just as they don't feel that way about the mayor or the governor or the President of the United States. I don't think they *ever* had such a feeling, at least not since they were toddlers. And as I looked at that inscription of my father's it occurred to me that our children don't have that sort of feeling of trust and belief in us parents because we adults no longer have that feeling of trust in any sort of authority ourselves. We haven't had it for a long time, I'd say, probably not since Eisenhower or since Kennedy was shot. And so we're unable to treat our children with the kind of certainty and authority that might make their lives seem as simple as ours once did."

THE END OF RESPECT

In *The War Between the Tates,* Alison Lurie describes a mother's chagrin when her son talks about his "fucking homework" and refers to his teacher as an "ass-kissing idiot." Yet it is not the bad language alone that distresses the fictional mother and countless real-life parents in America today. Children's dealings with their elders have suffered a true sea-change during the last two decades. While adults of the past could always say what they wanted, children were trained to hold back. Today it's Liberty Hall for young and old alike.

A fifth-grade teacher who grew up in the 1950s says: "Our attitudes towards adults in general were different when we were kids, and this bothers me a lot today as a parent and as a teacher. Kids don't necessarily respect you just because you're an adult or a parent or a teacher, the way we did. I mean, we had so much respect there was almost fear in it. Maybe it was too much, but I think there was something to be said for it. We looked up to adults, we trusted them, even the ones we disliked."

Another teacher, in charge of a sixth grade, observes: "When I was going to school, kids were much more accepting of authority. We would never have dreamed of contradicting our teachers! Now I find that everything always has to be substantiated. The kids are forever challenging everything I say. Sometimes I get the feeling that they are trying to score points, that they want to assert their position just so we teachers will see clearly that they have a right to say whatever they want. But when I was a student we didn't feel we had that right."

It is evident that the decline among children of automatic respect for adult authority has made teaching more challenging for the teacher. Using "child psychology," as many teachers used to do, requires first and foremost that there be a *child* to use it on. But many teachers are finding the children in their classroom far less likely to fall for the old stratagems—as little likely to be taken in, indeed, as any adult.

A fifth-grade teacher notes, on this subject: "You can't bluff with kids today. Ten years ago you used to be able to say, 'If you do that again I'm going to call your mother!' and chances were you never had to make that phone call. Now anything I say I know I'll have to come through, that they will challenge me, so I have to be careful. Today's kids are definitely less intimidatable. Maybe they know their mother isn't home and doesn't care *what* they do in school."

A fourth-grade teacher reports: "I remember about five or six years ago a kid here called his teacher a bitch and there was just a terrible to-do about it. He was suspended for a week—everybody was talking about it. Today we've adjusted our standards. We've simply gotten used to the new way kids talk, the way they just say anything they want. I suppose if a kid in my class called me a bitch I'd probably call his parents. But it still wouldn't be a big deal."

"Here's an example of what I consider disrespect," a New York public school teacher says. "We never would have thought of calling adults by their first names. But the kids in this school make it a point of finding out every teacher's first name. A few weeks ago my class suggested to me, 'Today we'll call you Norma, and you call us Miss and Mr. So and So.' They were shocked that I didn't agree to do it. They were serious about it. Or another small detail: when I went to school it was a big deal when the principal walked into the classroom.

Everybody practically stood at attention. Today when he comes into the class, the kids don't even stop talking."

Children themselves, without embarrassment, will provide examples of the disrespectful, almost contemptuous feeling they have for adults. Daniel, a friendly, mild-mannered ten-year-old growing up in Brewster, New York, describes an encounter he has had that morning with the school principal. "I can't stand Mr. Riley," Daniel says evenly, "because he makes everyone say 'Good morning, Mr. Riley' when you meet him in the hall. So when I met him this morning I said it, but real sarcastically, like this"—saying the words in an exaggerated, openly mocking singsong.

Children not long ago obviously shared some of Daniel's scorn for certain adults in their lives, but they repressed these feelings. The world of adults was a world apart, a world towards which they were required to maintain a certain deferential demeanor, a world, moreover, which they perceived, at least for the moment, to be superior to their own. It didn't oppress children growing up under the old hierarchical system to be forced to look at themselves as lower beings; every child knew with perfect certainty that this was temporary and that he would become an adult himself one day. For Daniel, however, the distance between the two worlds is far smaller. Based on the way adults have been treating him from an early age—based on his easy entry into the adult world via the television set that sits in his family's living room and kitchen and in his very own room—Daniel feels far more equal to adults than children felt in times past, even as recently as fifteen years ago. Being open about his disrespect for the school principal is so natural a consequence of his life's experience with the adult world that he is not even aware that anyone might consider it "wrong" or "bad" to behave that way.

Some of children's newly disrespectful attitude towards their teachers reflects a change in teachers' own attitudes towards authority. As writer and teacher Phillip Lopate explains: "There was a time when an anti-authority feeling among teachers was a valid reaction against a rigidly oppressive educational system. But today we've gone beyond that. Teachers seem to have lost faith in a certain natural authority they possess, a deserved authority that accrues to them simply because they know more and have something to teach."[1]

As teachers cease to trust their own authority and begin to treat their students on a more equal level, it is likely that children develop a more defensive, mistrustful, and disrespectful attitude towards them. The knowledge that the teacher may be wrong, so deliberately imparted to children by conscientious teachers today, does not necessarily make the child like and admire the teacher more for his honesty and friendliness; rather, it may cause the child to consider the teacher "just another one of the kids"—as unreliable and untrustworthy as he knows himself to be at his own stage of development.

The end of respect has broader ramifications than a change in adult-child relations. A connection may exist between the decline in respect for adult authority and the diminished role of religion in contemporary American life. A teacher in a New York parochial school, commenting about children's new reactions towards the authority of teachers, noted:

"The greatest problem with children's challenging and frequently disrespectful attitude towards authority is that it will make their religious lives more difficult. For every person there comes a point where there are certain questions that are impossible to answer. If you are going to follow a religion that believes in a higher being, then you have to accept the authority of that higher being without question. This must first be established in the relation between parent and child. If there isn't the properly respectful relation between parent and child, then the child will have trouble with authority figures generally, which will lead him to have trouble with his religious beliefs."

VERBAL ABUSE

The relation between children's disrespectful attitude towards adults and adults' abdication of authority may be seen in a phenomenon sufficiently common today to have become the basis of a study in the *American Journal of Psychiatry:* the "battered-parent syndrome."[2] In this latter-day reversal of the age-old practice of child abuse, children themselves become the physical aggressors in the family, brutalizing and terrorizing their parents. In such families, the authors of the study write, "the majority of the parents shy away from firmly stating that they, rather than the children, should set the rules, and some parents state that *everyone* should be equal." In an extreme example of parental abdication of authority, the parents of an eleven-year-old boy who had broken his mother's coccyx by pushing her into a door, then kicked her in the face while she was on the floor and lacerated her cheek, answered the interviewer's question whether they thought it was right or wrong for the child to behave violently towards his mother by saying, "It was neither right nor wrong."

While statistically few children actually assault their parents physically (fewer by far than the numbers of parents who batter their children), the numbers of families in which children are free to abuse their parents *verbally* are large indeed today. The freedom to express anger in words has become one of the sacred rights of American kids, an outlet that is believed to prevent the unhealthy build-up of smoldering, personality-distorting frustration. From the preschooler stamping his foot and shouting, "You're a mean, bad mommy and I hate you!" to the pithy deprecations of the teenager—"Don't be an asshole, Dad"—verbal abuse is regularly tolerated in great numbers of American families.

Until recently the regular expression of open aggression, be it physical or verbal, by a child towards a parent was unthinkable within the context of a normal family. Today's acceptance of what was once called "disrespect"—of rude and angry words from children to adults—may have helped to create a new attitude of disenchantment with childhood that is increasingly evident in American society. The signs of this antichild attitude may be seen not only in the proliferation of writings on "parents' rights" and "parents are people," in the increase in divorce cases in which *neither* parent wants custody of the children, in the indisputable increase in child abuse, child neglect, and child abandonment in many forms, but also symbolically, in such cultural manifestations as movies featuring evil children and books and movies about child torture, kidnapping, rape, and the like. As the study on the battered-parent syndrome concludes: "Rapid societal changes have made parental values and leadership less secure. Many parents today lean increasingly on health professionals for guidance in very basic child-rearing practices. The emphasis on youthful values and the neglect of the aged lead to an undermining of parental authority. . . . All of these factors can contribute to the reversal of generational hierarchies that we have described in parental battering."

Not only the reversal but the very removal of generational hierarchies, a trend that has its roots deep in American history but that has accelerated in recent years, may ultimately bode ill for both children and parents. As today's children grow less submissive and less agreeable, quite simply, than those children of the past who deferred and repressed their angers, parents grow more abusive, more neglectful, more likely to abandon rather than to nurture.

THE INTEGRATIONISTS

One way to gain perspective on the shrinking boundaries between childhood and adulthood and the new integration of children into adult society is to remember that it arose in the midst of the civil rights movement of the sixties and that it represents a similar challenge to traditional ways of thinking and behaving. The new awareness of injustice and oppression that was born in the sit-ins of Birmingham, the voter-registration campaigns, the confrontations at Selma, gradually sank into the American consciousness and changed the thinking of all but the most unregenerate racists and segregationists. Slowly, the civil rights movement widened its focus. Women were revealed for the first time as an oppressed minority (though not a minority in actual numbers). Homosexuals and finally children became causes. And just as the early manifestations of each of these movements shocked the general public and seemed to represent the ideas of a radical bunch of extremists—note, for instance, the widespread negative reaction among women towards the first women's liberation uprisings—so, gradually, the deeper changes that each movement sought to bring about came to seem reasonable and eventually inevitable even to those who resisted them most at the start. While the very idea of children's rights once seemed absurd to all but a small minority of radical students and counterculture dropouts in the sixties, it is noteworthy that the basic idea of the children's rights philosophy has come to be widely accepted today: that children are people, a notion that was sufficiently far-out twenty years ago to have become a shibboleth for the children's rights movement, but one that seems almost redundant in a time of unprecedented child power.

While children have not won the vote or gained the sort of political power that the libertarians of the sixties demanded, they *have* achieved a curious equality with adults, both within the family and in society at large, an equality that would have been as shocking in 1960 as the notion of letting children run for President still seems today. Whereas children, as a rule, were once a bit reticent in their dealings with adults, uncertain, reserved—"shy as a child," went the saying—today that shyness seems to have quite vanished.

A confirmation that children have changed in their dealings with adults was given in almost every one of the hundreds of interviews with fourth-, fifth-, sixth-, and seventh-graders that were held in preparation for this book. The directness, ease, confidence, and aplomb these children demonstrated again and again in their talks with an interviewer they had never met before were quite as surprising and indicative of change as anything they actually said. Neither boys nor girls were shy about discussing their social relations with the opposite sex, whether they "made out" or didn't, and how they felt about it. When eighth- and ninth-graders were being interviewed, it soon became clear that there was no need to pussyfoot about asking the once unaskable question "Are you a virgin?" No giggles or blushes but a rather casual "no" or an often rueful "yes" was the answer. Similarly, children of all ages spoke about their experiences with drugs and alcohol, all subjects that children of the past, if involved with illegal activities, would have been mum about. In fact, it often seemed that those children who seemed *less* casual and open, more reserved, came from homes that were more protective than today's norm. For protection is another dimension of a separatist rather than an integrationist approach towards child rearing. If you protect children from adult experiences, implied in your behavior is the presupposition that children must be treated differently than adults; ergo, a separation results. But what the rights movements of the sixties introduced was a *fear* of separation, of singling out any group, be it blacks or women or gays or Indians—or children. Just as "separate but equal" began to represent the worst sort of unfairness and bias, so too the singling out of children as a group to be treated differently, spoken to differently, dressed differently, and thought of as essentially different began to seem out of line with modern ways of thinking and behaving. Separation of children from the adult world came to seem old-fashioned, even intolerant.

THE END OF SECRECY

L E T T I N G   I T   A L L   H A N G   O U T

Once upon a time, in the Age of Protection, adult realities were purposely kept hidden from children. Today the formerly closed door between childhood and adulthood has been pushed ajar, sometimes torn from its hinges entirely.

The very fact that children seem more adult today has allowed grown-ups to let their hair down and relax with them in ways they were not able to do even half a generation ago. That familiar warning "Not in front of the children" is receding into the dim past to join the long-vanished injunction "Children should be seen and not heard." After all, there isn't a word or a phrase or an expletive an adult might inadvertently utter that could possibly surpass the language heard today on elementary school playgrounds. There is no aspect of adult life, be it promiscuity, perversity, dishonor, misery, or confusion, that seems outside the ken of today's children, certainly not those over the age of eight or nine.

The change from adult secretiveness to adult openness happened so swiftly and so pervasively that it almost covered up the traces of what came before. Weren't things always like this? People almost believe so. Only when adults take a moment to recall adult-child relations of their own childhoods do they recognize with a start that things were once very different indeed, and that a great part of this difference resides in the absence of adult reticence in the presence of children. Virtually nothing is hidden from children any longer.

Some of the new openness towards children may simply reflect a society-wide predilection for "letting it all hang out" and consequently a new willingness to tell the truth to children, especially

about those things parents once pretended they did "for your own good." As a Denver mother says: "When I was a child, everything was always supposedly done for *my* good. But today we're much more honest with our kids. I told my eight-year-old, 'I'm not sending you to bed at eight for *your* good. I'm doing this for *me!* You need to be in bed by eight because I need the space. I need the privacy.' "
Similarly, in a psychologically oriented era, parents are not averse to explaining their own motivations to their children. In this way, the former air of confidence and certainty that the adult world once carefully maintained before children has largely been abandoned. But some of the new adult openness towards children represents a deliberate change in attitude from protective to preparatory.

Author Judy Blume, through her books for children herself a pivotal figure in the transition from a secretive to an open approach, articulates the change to an interviewer: "I hate the idea that you should always protect children. They live in the same world we do. They see things and hear things. The worst is when there are secrets. . . . Sexuality and death—these are the two big secrets we try to keep from children, partly because the adult world isn't comfortable about them either. . . ."[1]

Blume's books illustrate her determination to end the practice of protecting children and withholding from them the facts of life and death. They were among the first to discuss openly aspects of sexuality such as masturbation and menstruation. But the appearance of adult matters in books or articles or programs aimed at children was by no means the primary reason secrecy declined; rather, it was an accommodation to the fact that it was no longer possible, in any case, to keep adult matters a secret from children, especially not the deep, dark secrets of sex.

In a society forbidding any public display of adult sexuality, it is easy to control children's exposure to the sexual side of adult life and maintain them at a high level of innocence. It was perhaps inevitable that the notable increase in sexual openness and liberality that occurred among adults in the 1960s—that gradual weakening of taboos and rapid lowering of restrictions that came to be known as the sexual revolution—was accompanied by a simultaneous decline in reticence about sex towards children. As adults under the leadership of the

"Woodstock Generation" began to allow sex more public visibility than it had had in centuries, by conducting their sexual affairs more conspicuously in public places, by allowing explicit sexual matters to appear in books and movies and eventually on television, it became hard to limit this material to adult eyes and ears only. Soon people began to consider that perhaps this end of secrecy was a good thing —"If you can't beat 'em, join 'em." The secrecy of the past began to seem unnecessary, if not positively misguided.

BREAKTHROUGH BOOKS

In the Golden Age of Innocence, children read books about fairies and animals, or about other children engaged in the carefree pleasures of childhood. Today children are likely to be reading a very different kind of children's book. Here, in summary, is a children's book published several years ago by a major publisher:

> A beautiful girl of fourteen lives in a small town where her father is a barber and her mother a humble laundress. The girl dreams of romance and fame but is obliged to spend her days in drudgery, cleaning houses and baby-sitting. At last she decides to run away from home and seek her fortune in the big city.

So far the story resembles the familiar tales of the past. But it continues:

> On her first day in the big city, she meets a handsome man, who befriends her when she is lost. She falls in love with him. But, alas, he turns out to be a pimp. He compels her to become one of his prostitutes. At first she is appalled at what has befallen her. She cannot believe that she has to "do it" with all sorts of strange men. But soon, out of love for her protector, she becomes one of his most successful hookers. She becomes the pimp's favorite, which arouses the jealousy of her colleagues. One of the other girls puts LSD into our heroine's soft drink and she has a bad trip. Finally, after many bad adventures she finds her way into a rehabilitation center for

runaway children. There she gets "therapy" and prepares to return to her small home town, a sadder and wiser girl.[2]

This book, widely read by ten-, eleven-, and twelve-year-olds a few years ago, is an example—by no means an extreme one—of a genre of children's books published in increasing numbers during the last fifteen years. These are books that deal with subjects heretofore considered unsuitable for children—books that are often called "breakthrough" books or "the new realism."

The first real "breakthrough" book was probably a small volume for young children by John Donovan published in the late 1960s.[3] *I'll Get There, It Better Be Worth the Trip* is a simple story about a boy, his best friend, and his dog. The uproar occasioned by this book centered on a brief scene in which two nine-year-old boys who are having a sleepover at one of their houses are suddenly drawn to each other and find, to their surprise, that they are kissing. A homosexual episode in a children's book, though so carefully and subtly presented that many readers totally overlooked it, represents far more than increased openness about sex. Donovan's book heralded a change in attitude towards children, a sign that a decision had been made by influential cultural forces to end a period of vestigial Victorianism that had long served to protect children from certain realities of life. Instead, in the years to come, books were to serve a new function: to prepare children, from an early age, for life's complexities and dangers.

MAD MAGAZINE

There was once a time when children believed that adults were inevitably good, that all presidents were as honest as Abe Lincoln, that their parents' world was wiser and better than their own child world, a time when children were expected to give up their seats to adults in public conveyances, to reserve strong language for the company of their peers, and in every way to treat adults with "respect." Then along came *Mad* magazine. If there is a single cultural force in the last twenty-five years epitomizing the change that has overtaken childhood, it is that singular publication.

When *Mad* first appeared in the early fifties it was an offshoot of the principal medium of popular child culture of the day—comics. It had a comic-book format, with stories told by cartoon figures speaking via word-filled balloons above their heads. But while comic books of earlier years ran the gamut from "cute" Walt Disney types to the gruesome "Tale of the Crypt" variety of horror comics, nevertheless they all belonged to the category of fantasy, long an accepted adjunct of childhood. Then *Mad* introduced a new element: satire. Before *Mad*, satire traditionally entered young people's lives in late adolescence, often via college humor magazines. *Mad* was the first satirical magazine for children, a sort of Swift for Kids, dealing with children's own reality—their parents, school, and culture—in an irreverent and mocking way. Its readership has grown ever younger, from high-school-age kids in the sixties to nine- and ten-year-olds today.

In the first years, *Mad*'s sharp satirical lance was aimed at the cultural media children were exposed to—old classics, comics, radio, movies, and, with increasing frequency, television. Action comic strips of the *Superman* variety were ridiculed in a feature called "Superduper Man." "Prince Violent" mocked the pseudo-historical genre of comic strip. "Dragged Net" laughed at the "real-life" police dramas that were popular on the radio in the fifties. As television began to take up more of children's free time, a procession of parodies of TV programs and especially commercials began to appear. "From the gaudy grille of Ca-dil-lac to the fins of Che-vro-let. We will push GM's new mo-dels and make obso-les-cence pay!" ran a parody in the late fifties. By 1960 television's pre-eminent position in children's lives was noted by *Mad:* in "A Checklist for Baby-Sitters," the most important consideration for whether to take the job was the condition of the television set. Food, baby-sitting rates, and record player follow shortly. In the last position, as number 10, was the type and number of children to be cared for.

While writers for *Mad* in its first decade chose mainly cultural material to satirize, from the mid-sixties on the focus turned more and more to the child's social environment: parents and the family as an institution. Parents were appalled at the mocking, disrespectful attitude the magazine seemed to encourage towards adults; children adored it, soaked it up like sponges. A feature entitled "If Babies Could Take Parent Pictures," for instance, captions one of its illustrations: "Here's my idiot father trying to drive and take pictures at the same time. I was lucky to get home alive." The phrase "My idiot father" hardly has a jarring sound in the 1980s when much of what kids say to adults is unprintable, but in 1960 the words were shocking. At some point during those two decades a long-established convention came to an end, one that had compelled children to repress their anger and impatience, forcing them to mutter under their breath, perhaps, but rarely allowing them to be openly abusive towards adults. *Mad* magazine may have been more influential in the move towards free expression among children than has heretofore been acknowledged.

As Al Feldstein, editor-in-chief of *Mad* for the past twenty-five years (sometimes known as Chief Madman), describes the change:

"What we did was to take the absurdities of the adult world and show kids that adults are not omnipotent. That their parents were being two-faced in their standards—telling kids to be honest, not to lie, and yet themselves cheating on their income tax. We showed kids that the world out there is unfair, that a lot of people out there are lying to them, cheating them. We told them there's a lot of garbage out in the world and you've got to be aware of it. Everything you read in the papers is not necessarily true. What you see on television is mostly lies. You're going to have to learn to think for yourself."[4]

A relentless parade of features exposing parental hypocrisies caused shock-waves of admiration to reverberate among *Mad*'s young readers (who were not unaware of their older siblings' embattled protests against the more profound hypocrisies of the Great Society as it engaged in the Vietnam "conflict"). For example, a regular feature of the mid-sixties entitled "What They Say and What It Really Means" portrays a mother and father addressing their teenage daughter and her seedy-looking boyfriend: "We have nothing against the boy, darling," is What They Say. "It's just that you're both so terribly young." Then the writers spell out What It Really

Means: "Wait until you find a boy of your own religion who's got money"—parental bigotry and venality and hypocrisy knocked down in one fell swoop.

As the sixties wore on towards the seventies and adult culture grew increasingly sophisticated and sexually open, *Mad*'s parodies grew ever more adult themselves, dealing more and more often with adult sexuality, women's liberation, the drug and alcohol scene, and other unchildlike subjects. Movie satires abandoned Walt Disney and appeared with titles such as "Boob and Carnal and Alas and Alfred." A take-off on the song "Matchmaker" from the musical *Fiddler on the Roof* was called "Headshrinker" and included such lines as "I'm Sheila, a free-sex fanatic, I'm Nancy, a speed freak just now, I'm Joy, who makes bombs in the attic, and answers the phone with quotations from Mao," and ended prophetically, "Headshrinker, headshrinker, this is our fate, kids we can't stand, parents we hate."

Child readers of the mid-1970s were now swept along in adult society's increasing preoccupation with sex. "Mom and I are proud of you," says a parent to a teenage daughter in a feature of the 1970s. "We heard that you and Steve were the only students in the history of your college who didn't go to bed together on your first date." The daughter answers via a balloon above her head: "That's true, Dad. But we did make out on a couch, on the floor, etc."

As divorce began to reach epidemic proportions in the second half of the 1970s, *Mad* did not fail to comment on it. A 1975 parody called "Broken Homes and Gardens" had a mother and father who declared that they *weren't* going to get a divorce. "Because of the kids," they explained. "Neither of us wants them." In 1976 appeared "Unweddings of the Future," in which invitations were sent out by the parents of the soon-to-be-ex-bride.

Comparing an issue of *Mad* of the 1980s with one from the 1950s provides an almost shocking view of the change that childhood had undergone in those years. The magazine of December 1980, for example, features a parody of the movie *Little Darlings,* a film about two thirteen-year-old girls at summer camp who have a race to see which of them can lose her virginity first. The *Mad* version includes an outdoor salesman hawking a new kind of children's wares: "Get your training diaphragms here!" he cries. "She's starting foreplay now," a little girl observes as she spies on a pair of prospective mini-lovers. When one of the pubescent heroines gets cold feet during her final seduction scene, her gangly swain protests, "I'm getting frustrated! Y'know, there are NAMES for girls like you!" His partner asks, "Is Crazy Teenager one of them?" He replies, "No . . . but you got the INITIALS right!!!" Will *Mad*'s child readership "get" the allusion? An informal survey of several average seventh-graders suggests that the CT epithet is well known to that age group today.

An ironic footnote: *Little Darlings* received an R rating, officially barring admission to unaccompanied children under seventeen—that is, to almost all *Mad*'s readership. Nevertheless great numbers of pre-teenagers gained access to *Little Darlings*, as they do to many other R movies.

It is almost impossible to imagine children of 1955 openly reading about diaphragms and foreplay. But that was still the Golden Age of Innocence. One of the reasons it was so much easier to maintain children in that special state twenty-five years ago, and why it is impossible to bring it back today, is precisely because in those days movies like *Little Darlings* did not exist.

THE MOVIES GROW UP

When children took off for the movies not so long ago, their parents never gave a moment's thought to whether the film might contain scenes of nudity, gang rape, homosexuality, or sadistic violence. This is not because parents were more casual in the good old days, but rather because virtually *all* American films made before 1955 were suitable for child consumption. The situation was almost a complete reversal of today's, when the great majority of films children see contain adult material; then, innocence was imposed on adult film viewers. A rigid, prudish motion-picture production code, in effect until the early sixties, kept nearly all aspects of adult sexuality, all strong or blasphemous language, and all excessive violence out of films altogether.

When the liberating waves of change in the sixties created a greater acceptance of sexual material among the general public, the film world took swift advantage to slough off the rigid rules of the past and begin including more adult subjects in their products. Though the production code continued to exist for a number of years, films began to be released without its approval and were still able to reach a wide audience, including children. Suddenly, the floodgates were opened and sex was everywhere. Parents were appalled to find that their "innocent" children were losing their innocence rapidly.

Books, too, which had been subject to equally repressive strictures in the years before the sixties, now began to include sexual scenes and long-forbidden four-letter words in their pages. But this had less of a direct impact on children than the new adultness of the movies. The visual media have always been more accessible to children at all stages of cognitive development than the written word. While the verbal description of a relationship, let us say an explicitly sexual one, might tax the intellect of an eight- or nine-year-old, a visual representation of it is far more likely to sustain a child's attention and make a deep impression.

To be sure, even in the Golden Age of Innocence of the 1930s and 1940s, children had not been completely protected from damaging experiences in their movie-going. Since parental anxieties about childhood innocence in America once centered almost exclusively on sexuality, adults failed to notice a strong streak of violence that, paradoxically, pervaded those very films made especially for children, even while the vast number made for adults were violence-free. Critic Nora Sayre recalls cowering under her seat in the movie theater during much of *Snow White* and *The Wizard of Oz*, two of the most famous children's movies of the past. Many adults recall the forest-fire scene in Disney's *Bambi* as one of the traumatic events of their childhood. (Not surprisingly, most of these disturbing movie scenes featured the loss of a parent.) Meanwhile, the swashbuckling costume dramas, the musicals with June Allyson or Esther Williams, the Jerry Lewis and Dean Martin comedies of the late 1940s and 1950s, though considered adult films in their day, remain the most supremely innocent movies ever made.

There were also the horror movies and the gangster films of the thirties, forties, and fifties, bringing their share of unchildlike terror to any child in the audience. But the level of violence in even the most sordid grade B movies never approached the excesses of death and mutilation that have come to be common in films of the last ten years. The *scale* of mayhem was smaller in the past. The production code prevented the camera from lingering in a loving way on the actual moment of ultimate violence, and the blood was never in "living technicolor," as it was to appear on the television news reports of real-life violence in Vietnam in later years, and in so many popular films of the seventies and eighties such as *The Godfather* or *Apocalypse Now,* to name two out of hundreds. And in any case, though children were not barred from seeing the more adult-oriented movies of the past, they were generally more attracted to the big-budget Hollywood musicals and comedies that were also available in those years. Today, however, violent movies are often made appealing to children by the inclusion of elements highly attractive to a pre-teenage audience: the dancing and music in a film such as *Saturday Night Fever,* or the especially enticing presence of a child star in *The Exorcist* or *The Shining.*

When all movies were as pure as Ivory Snow, children were free to see any movie they wished. There was no serious need for parents to exercise any cultural repressiveness in regard to their children. But as films grew more openly sexual and violent in the late sixties and early seventies, groups of parents, educators, and religious leaders began to protest against the inclusion of such material. The film industry found itself facing the alternatives of a stricter censorship code that would remove, once again, all controversial material from films or some sort of classification system to differentiate between those films containing adult material and those suitable for children's viewing. Not surprisingly, the industry exercised the latter option and in 1963 devised a rating system that evolved into the one in operation today, which bars children under seventeen from films rated X, and limits the access of children under sixteen to films rated R by insisting that they be accompanied by an adult. Children are allowed free entry into films rated G and PG, although parents are warned that the PG-rated films may contain some material unsuitable for young children.

The movie industry breathed a sigh of relief with the successful transition from an industry-wide production code limiting all films to a level of innocence suitable for children to a differential rating system allowing film makers far greater artistic latitude. Under the new system, parents were expected to be guided by the assigned ratings and to protect their children as they saw fit. Thus, without any new parental restrictiveness required, children were now supposed to be protected by theater owners from seeing the most sexually explicit or violent films, those rated R or X.

But the rating system did not prove to carry the protective clout it promised when it was introduced. Aside from the great numbers of parents who, whether from lack of baby-sitters at home or for other reasons, took their children along to see R movies *they* wanted to see, it became clear that unescorted children were easily gaining access to R-rated films, either by latching on to unrelated adults or, in many cases, through the complete disregard of restrictions by theater owners. In 1974, when *The Exorcist* opened in Washington, D.C., with an R rating, a newspaper critic commented on the number of children, many as young as six and eight, who had been brought to see the picture or who had managed to get an adult in the line to take them in. Even the X rating, apparently, is far from inviolable. Recently a number of fourteen- and fifteen-year-olds reported to an interviewer that they had little trouble gaining admission to the X-rated film *Caligula*.

The Rating Board, regardless of its effectiveness, was in any case never a protective agency for the preservation of childhood innocence. Its function, as described by its current chairman, Richard Heffner, is to "reflect standards, not set them," thus putting it somewhat in the category of *Mad* magazine, which also purports to reflect rather than establish moral codes. The mandate of the Rating Board is, rather, to rate each film according to how the board perceives the average parent might judge it with regard to his own children. And how does the Rating Board discover what accurately represents the majority opinion? By observing the reaction of parents to the ratings *after* the film is shown at local theaters. If the film exhibitors report that angry parents are protesting a film's ratings, then the board moves to adjust its rating policies thereafter. "We try to feel the parental pulse," Heffner explains. "If we're doing the wrong thing, we'll hear about it quickly."[5]

The parental pulse, however, seems to have grown sluggish in recent years. Reflecting adult standards in an era of relaxed sexual prohibitions, the board has become increasingly lenient about the inclusion of sexual material in films it dubs PG. "A nipple won't automatically make a film an R as it used to," says Heffner. Similarly, the inclusion in film dialogue of some long-forbidden expletives no longer ensures an uncontested R rating.

If the rating system is simply a reflection of parental attitudes, then it appears that today's parents, many of them former peace marchers and antiwar protesters, condone a considerable amount of violence as well. In 1981, *Raiders of the Lost Ark* received a PG rating in spite of more than sixty deaths by gun, poison dart, propeller blade, knives, and other means, as well as a pit filled with deadly snakes and a beautiful heroine threatened with a red-hot branding iron. "I did have a lot of problems with that film," Heffner allowed, "but we're ·not here to impose our moral standards on the public. We're not censors. We try to make educated guesses about what most parents feel. We only ask one question. 'Would most parents in America want their kids to be *prevented* from seeing this particular film unless they were accompanied by an adult?' "

Probably not, no matter *what* the film. Odds are that most parents today would not feel obliged to accompany their ten- or eleven-year-olds to the movies in order to mitigate a potentially confusing or upsetting experience. The protective urge that parents once felt so strongly, the feeling that exposure to frightening images, to violence, to explicit sex, would somehow be harmful to children, has faded. The pragmatic attitude of today's parents might be spelled out approximately thus: "We live in a violent society. The kids see huge amounts of violence on TV in any case, as well as all sorts of sexual matters. There's no way of protecting them from these realities. And besides, they're *eleven years old!* It's not as if they were vulnerable toddlers!"

And so they send the kids off to *Raiders* with the hideous deaths, or *All That Jazz*, with its graphic erotic fantasy sequence, or *Little Darlings*, with its defloration compulsion, or *Kramer vs. Kramer*, with its theme of maternal abandonment and parental ineptitude. After all, parents explain, it's unrealistic to be worrying about what the kids see in movies when *real life* carries so many more *real dangers*—drugs and pregnancy and rape and murder, to say nothing of war and possible nuclear destruction of the entire species!

In less than two decades we have seen a great cultural change in the movie industry. Today the majority of films being released deal with mature subject matter that would have seemed unsuitable for children a generation ago. And yet children view these films regularly. Now, as they show signs that they have been influenced by their regular viewing of "adult" movies, society is forced to confront the implication of that cultural change: some of the lines of demarcation between childhood and adulthood are being removed as children look, talk, and behave in ways that do not seem very childlike. For when all movies were limited to innocuous material and children were kept innocent, adults nonetheless *knew* those things that movies were not allowed to show and behaved in ways that movies were not allowed to portray. Today the kids know too. And their behavior often reflects that knowledge.

CONFRONTING ADULT UNHAPPINESS

Without a doubt the end of adult secrecy reflects a deep shift in thinking about children and childhood. Children these days are often deliberately exposed to adult unhappiness and adult frailty, in the hope that early awareness will help them deal with the inevitable problems of adulthood that lie ahead.

Motivated by just such a belief, in June 1979 writer and teacher Phillip Lopate undertook to put on a production of Chekhov's tragedy *Uncle Vanya* with a group of ten-, eleven-, and twelve-year-old students at P.S. 75 in Manhattan.[6] "I wanted to see what would happen when the children were forced to confront adult unhappiness," Lopate explains. "I think they are doing this to a great degree in real life, and I think such an experience as putting on *Uncle Vanya* can be helpful to prepare children to understand that adults *can* waste their lives, to understand that at an early age. How else will children know that they mustn't squander their lives, that they must seize their own time more effectively?" But besides revealing some of the complexities of adult life, Lopate believes that the children's exposure to Chekhov's drama may have also made them aware of some of the ways that adult life resembles their own. "The play is about adult futility and boredom," he observes. "And I was surprised at how well the children connected to it. Because in a way they're waiting for their lives to begin. So there turned out to be much more of a connection between Chekhov and childhood than I had ever thought there would be."

This indoctrination of children into the former secrets of adult life cannot help but make children feel differently about themselves and adults; as they grow less trusting and dependent, they feel themselves more equal, somehow. The result of this manifestly changed attitude is that children seem older than their counterparts of the past. The author of a book about children brought up on communes observes such an effect among children who took part in a weekly communal "group-gripe," a problem-solving session. Admiring the aplomb of a nine-year-old girl who listened to her mother discuss in public her various problems, including those pertaining to her relationship with her daughter, the author notes: "She was aware of her mother's effect on her, of her mother's designs on her, in a way that made her seem older than her nine years. It wasn't the freedom of speech that was impressive. It was a kind of emotional distance which allowed Karen [the nine-year-old] to see her mother as a person, to unravel the mystery of her parents a little earlier than some of us who began to do it when we went to college."[7]

Like the children raised in counterculture communes, children of divorce find themselves propelled into the adult world with greater force than those in ordinary two-parent families. Yet even children from the most stable households are far more privy to adult grief and disorder than children were a generation ago, thanks to television and thanks to the greater inclination of adults today to level with their kids. The impact of this knowledge of adult woe, however, may be different for children in different family circumstances—and especially affecting for the children of divorce.

CRITICAL POWERS TOO EARLY AWAKENED

Most children learn the facts (or fictions) of adult sexuality at an early age in a sexually liberated culture such as ours. But there is a great difference between knowing about sex from movies and television and applying this knowledge to *one's own parents*. In intact families, a diminishing breed today, children seem to disassociate their quite comprehensive body of sexual knowledge from those adults most important in their lives: their parents. Thus a nine-year-old boy who talks glibly about sexual intercourse, homosexuality, abortion, and rape recently revealed to an interviewer that he still clings to the belief that his own parents have actually had sexual intercourse—he used a cruder word—only two times in all, the number required to produce his sister and himself. In spite of all the scenes of sexual hyperactivity, lust, and adultery that he has viewed on television and in the movies, he has chosen to believe that none of it applies to his own mother and father.

It may be that the various sordid or violent sexual matters that children are exposed to in the media today leave less of a mark on a child's spirit than observers imagine, so long as nothing connects the extrinsic material with his crucial inner circle of parents, siblings, and himself. But for the children of divorce, the old secrets of parental sexuality are hard to hide. Now they must relate the confusing and often frightening actions they have been watching on television screens for so many years to their own parents.

Once children put it all together with their own family, they become far more vulnerable to those outside influences. As Anna Freud wrote of a child involved in parental acrimony during a divorce: "His confidence is shattered by his critical powers being too early awakened." She went on to consider the consequences of such an early awakening: "He acts like an employee in a bankrupt firm who has lost all confidence in his principals and no longer therefore feels any pleasure in his work. Thus the child in such circumstances stops work—that is, his normal development is checked and he reacts to the abnormal conditions in some abnormal way."[8]

Child experts today often observe the connection between the child's "critical powers being too early awakened" as a result of divorce and his subsequent vulnerability to overstimulation via the cultural media. Katharine Rees, a child psychoanalyst, notes that "the more stable a child's home life and the more satisfactory the home models, the less affected the child seems to be by TV or movie sex and violence." Dr. Paulina F. Kernberg, director of child and adolescent psychiatry at the Westchester Division of New York Hospital–Cornell Medical Center, agrees: "Children's difficulties today are less a matter of overstimulation by what they see on television and more a result of a deficit in family structure. Children sense a difference when something is just a picture on TV, and when it conforms with some sort of reality they have observed themselves. Seeing programs on TV doesn't explain children's precocious and unchildlike behavior as much as the lack of the structure of marital ties and of clear parental roles."[9] A school psychologist in Denver reports: "The children I meet who are most affected by TV have other family problems as well. If they're already vulnerable, then they don't seem to be able to handle the TV sex and violence. They can't differentiate between the TV world and the real world."

Parents have long taken comfort in the thought that children are not necessarily damaged by exposure to information or even experiences that are over their heads because "they will only absorb as much as they are ready for." This belief may very well have had validity for those children of the past who grew up in a stable, secure, and protected environment. But children growing up otherwise, whose critical powers are indeed being prematurely awakened, may be ready for all the horrors they might be exposed to. It all connects, sadly enough, with their own lives.

*T*HE END OF PLAY

*O*f all the changes that have altered the topography of
childhood, the most dramatic has been the disappearance of childhood play. Whereas a decade or two ago children were easily distinguished from the adult world by the very nature of their play, today
children's occupations do not differ greatly from adult diversions.

Infants and toddlers, to be sure, continue to follow certain timeless
patterns of manipulation and exploration; adolescents, too, have not
changed their free-time habits so very much, turning as they ever
have towards adult pastimes and amusements in their drive for autonomy, self-mastery, and sexual discovery. It is among the ranks of
school-age children, those six-to-twelve-year-olds who once avidly
filled their free moments with childhood play, that the greatest
change is evident. In the place of traditional, sometimes ancient
childhood games that were still popular a generation ago, in the place
of fantasy and make-believe play—"You be the mommy and I'll be
the daddy"—doll play or toy-soldier play, jump-rope play, ball-
bouncing play, today's children have substituted television viewing
and, most recently, video games.

Many parents have misgivings about the influence of television.
They sense that a steady and time-consuming exposure to passive
entertainment might damage the ability to play imaginatively and
resourcefully, or prevent this ability from developing in the first
place. A mother of two school-age children recalls: "When I was
growing up, we used to go out into the vacant lots and make up
week-long dramas and sagas. This was during third, fourth, fifth
grades. But my own kids have never done that sort of thing, and

somehow it bothers me. I wish we had cut down on the TV years ago, and maybe the kids would have learned how to play."

The testimony of parents who eliminate television for periods of time strengthens the connection between children's television watching and changed play patterns. Many parents discover that when their children don't have television to fill their free time, they resort to the old kinds of imaginative, traditional "children's play." Moreover, these parents often observe that under such circumstances "they begin to seem more like children" or "they act more childlike." Clearly, a part of the definition of childhood, in adults' minds, resides in the nature of children's play.

Children themselves sometimes recognize the link between play and their own special definition as children. In an interview about children's books with four ten-year-old girls, one of them said: "I read this story about a girl my age growing up twenty years ago— you know, in 1960 or so—and she seemed so much younger than me in her behavior. Like she might be playing with dolls, or playing all sorts of children's games, or jump-roping or something." The other girls all agreed that they had noticed a similar discrepancy between themselves and fictional children in books of the past: those children seemed more like children. "So what do *you* do in your spare time, if you don't play with dolls or play make-believe games or jump rope or do things kids did twenty years ago?" they were asked. They laughed and answered, "We watch TV."

But perhaps other societal factors have caused children to give up play. Children's greater exposure to adult realities, their knowledge of adult sexuality, for instance, might make them more sophisticated, less likely to play like children. Evidence from the counterculture communes of the sixties and seventies adds weight to the argument that it is television above all that has eliminated children's play. Studies of children raised in a variety of such communes, all television-free, showed the little communards continuing to fill their time with those forms of play that have all but vanished from the lives of conventionally reared American children. And yet these counterculture kids were casually exposed to all sorts of adult matters—drug taking, sexual intercourse. Indeed, they sometimes incorporated these matters into their play: "We're mating," a pair of six-year-olds told a reporter to explain their curious bumps and grinds. Nevertheless, to all observers the commune children preserved a distinctly childlike and even innocent demeanor, an impression that was produced mainly by the fact that they spent most of their time playing. Their play defined them as belonging to a special world of childhood.

Not all children have lost the desire to engage in the old-style childhood play. But so long as the most popular, most dominant members of the peer group, who are often the most socially precocious, are "beyond" playing, then a common desire to conform makes it harder for those children who still have the drive to play to go ahead and do so. Parents often report that their children seem ashamed of previously common forms of play and hide their involvement with such play from their peers. "My fifth-grader still plays with dolls," a mother tells, "but she keeps them hidden in the basement where nobody will see them." This social check on the play instinct serves to hasten the end of childhood for even the least advanced children.

What seems to have replaced play in the lives of great numbers of preadolescents these days, starting as early as fourth grade, is a burgeoning interest in boy-girl interactions—"going out" or "going together." These activities do not necessarily involve going anywhere or doing anything sexual, but nevertheless are the first stage of a sexual process that used to commence at puberty or even later. Those more sophisticated children who are already involved in such manifestly unchildlike interests make plain their low opinion of their peers who still *play*. "Some of the kids in the class are real weird," a fifth-grade boy states. "They're not interested in going out, just in trucks and stuff, or games pretending they're monsters. Some of them don't even *try* to be cool."

VIDEO GAMES VERSUS MARBLES

Is there really any great difference, one might ask, between that gang of kids playing video games by the hour at their local candy store these days and those small fry who used to hang around together spending equal amounts of time playing marbles? It is easy to see a similarity between the two activities: each requires a certain amount of manual dexterity, each is almost as much fun to watch as to play, each is simple and yet challenging enough for that middle-childhood age group for whom time can be so oppressive if unfilled.

One significant difference between the modern pre-teen fad of video games and the once popular but now almost extinct pastime of marbles is economic: playing video games costs twenty-five cents for approximately three minutes of play; playing marbles, after a small initial investment, is free. The children who frequent video-game machines require a considerable outlay of quarters to subsidize their fun; two, three, or four dollars is not an unusual expenditure for an eight- or nine-year-old spending an hour or two with his friends playing Asteroids or Pac-Man or Space Invaders. For most of the children the money comes from their weekly allowance. Some augment this amount by enterprising commercial ventures—trading and selling comic books, or doing chores around the house for extra money.

But what difference does it make *where* the money comes from? Why should that make video games any less satisfactory as an amusement for children? In fact, having to pay for the entertainment, whatever the source of the money, and having its duration limited by one's financial resources changes the nature of the game, in a subtle way diminishing the satisfactions it offers. Money and time become intertwined, as they so often are in the adult world and as, in the past, they almost never were in the child's world. For the child playing marbles, meanwhile, time has a far more carefree quality, bounded only by the requirements to be home by suppertime or by dark.

But the video-game-playing child has an additional burden—a burden of choice, of knowing that the money used for playing Pac-Man could have been saved for Christmas, could have been used to buy something tangible, perhaps something "worthwhile," as his parents might say, rather than being "wasted" on video games. There is a certain sense of adultness that spending money imparts, a feeling of being a consumer, which distinguishes a game with a price from its counterparts among the traditional childhood games children once played at no cost.

There are other differences as well. Unlike child-initiated and child-organized games such as marbles, video games are adult-created mechanisms not entirely within the child's control, and thus less likely to impart a sense of mastery and fulfillment: the coin may get jammed, the machine may go haywire, the little blobs may stop eating the funny little dots. Then the child must go to the storekeeper to complain, to get his money back. He may be "ripped off" and simply lose his quarter, much as his parents are when they buy a faulty applicance. This possibility of disaster gives the childs play a certain weight that marbles never imposed on its light-hearted players.

Even if a child has a video game at home requiring no coin outlay, the play it provides is less than optimal. The noise level of the machine is high—too high, usually, for the child to conduct a conversation easily with another child. And yet, according to its enthusiasts, this very noisiness is a part of the game's attraction. The loud whizzes, crashes, and whirrs of the video-game machine "blow the mind" and create an excitement that is quite apart from the excitement generated simply by trying to win a game. A traditional childhood game such as marbles, on the other hand, has little built-in stimulation; the excitement of playing is generated entirely by the players' own actions. And while the pace of a game of marbles is close to the child's natural physiological rhythms, the frenzied activities of video games serve to "rev up" the child in an artificial way, almost in the way a stimulant or an amphetamine might. Meanwhile the perceptual impact of a video game is similar to that of watching television—the action, after all, takes place on a television screen—causing the eye to defocus slightly and creating a certain alteration in the child's natural state of consciousness.

Parents' instinctive reaction to their children's involvement with video games provides another clue to the difference between this contemporary form of play and the more traditional pastimes such as marbles. While parents, indeed most adults, derive open pleasure from watching children at play, most parents today are not delighted to watch their kids flicking away at the Pac-Man machine. This does not seem to them to be real play. As a mother of two school-age children anxiously explains, "We used to do real childhood sorts of things when I was a kid. We'd build forts and put on crazy plays and make up new languages, and just generally we *played*. But today my kids don't play that way at all. They like video games and of course they still go in for sports outdoors. They go roller skating and ice skating and skiing and all. But they don't seem to really *play.*"

Some of this feeling may represent a certain nostalgia for the past and the old generation's resistance to the different ways of the new. But it is more likely that most adults have an instinctive understanding of the importance of play in their own childhood. This feeling stokes their fears that their children are being deprived of something irreplaceable when they flip the levers on the video machines to manipulate the electronic images rather than flick their fingers to send a marble shooting towards another marble.

PLAY DEPRIVATION

In addition to television's influence, some parents and teachers ascribe children's diminished drive to play to recent changes in the school curriculum, especially in the early grades.

"Kindergarten, traditionally a playful port of entry into formal school, is becoming more academic, with children being taught specific skills, taking tests, and occasionally even having homework," begins a report on new directions in early childhood education.[1] Since 1970, according to the United States census, the proportion of three- and four-year-olds enrolled in school has risen dramatically, from 20.5 percent to 36.7 percent in 1980, and these nursery schools have largely joined the push towards academic acceleration in the early grades. Moreover, middle-class nursery schools in recent years have introduced substantial doses of academic material into their daily programs, often using those particular devices originally intended to help culturally deprived preschoolers in compensatory programs such as Headstart to catch up with their middle-class peers. Indeed, some of the increased focus on academic skills in nursery schools and kindergartens is related to the widespread popularity among young children and their parents of *Sesame Street,* a program originally intended to help deprived children attain academic skills, but universally watched by middle-class toddlers as well.

Parents of the *Sesame Street* generation often demand a "serious," skill-centered program for their preschoolers in school, afraid that the old-fashioned, play-centered curriculum will bore their alphabet-spouting, number-chanting four- and five-year-olds. A few parents, especially those whose children have not attended television classes or nursery school, complain of the high-powered pace of kindergarten these days. A father whose five-year-old daughter attends a public kindergarten declares: "There's a lot more pressure put on little kids these days than when we were kids, that's for sure. My daughter never went to nursery school and never watched *Sesame,* and she had a lot of trouble when she entered kindergarten this fall. By October, just a month and a half into the program, she was already flunking. The teacher told us our daughter couldn't keep up with the other kids. And believe me, she's a bright kid! All the other kids were getting gold stars and smiley faces for their work, and every day Emily would come home in tears because she didn't get a gold star. Remember when we were in kindergarten? We were *children* then. We were allowed just to play!"

A kindergarten teacher confirms the trend towards early academic pressure. "We're expected by the dictates of the school system to push a lot of curriculum," she explains. "Kids in our kindergarten can't sit around playing with blocks any more. We've just managed to squeeze in one hour of free play a week, on Fridays."

The diminished emphasis on fantasy and play and imaginative activities in early childhood education and the increased focus on early academic-skill acquisition have helped to change childhood from a play-centered time of life to one more closely resembling the style of adulthood: purposeful, success-centered, competitive. The likelihood is that these preschool "workers" will not metamorphose back into players when they move on to grade school. This decline in play is surely one of the reasons why so many teachers today comment that their third- or fourth-graders act like tired business-men instead of like children.

What might be the consequences of this change in children's play? Children's propensity to engage in that extraordinary series of behaviors characterized as "play" is perhaps the single great dividing line between childhood and adulthood, and has probably been so throughout history. The make-believe games anthropologists have recorded of children in primitive societies around the world attest to the universality of play and to the uniqueness of this activity to the immature members of each society. But in those societies, and probably in Western society before the middle or late eighteenth century, there was always a certain similarity between children's play and adult work. The child's imaginative play took the form of imitation of various aspects of adult life, culminating in the gradual transformation of the child's play from make-believe work to *real* work. At this point, in primitive societies or in our own society of the past, the child took her or his place in the adult work world and the distinctions between adulthood and childhood virtually vanished. But in today's technologically advanced society there is no place for the child in the adult work world. There are not enough jobs, even of the most menial kind, to go around for adults, much less for children. The child must continue to be dependent on adults for many years while gaining the knowledge and skills necessary to become a working member of society.

This is not a new situation for children. For centuries children have endured a prolonged period of dependence long after the helplessness of early childhood is over. But until recent years children remained childlike and playful far longer than they do today. Kept isolated from the adult world as a result of deliberate secrecy and protectiveness, they continued to find pleasure in socially sanctioned childish activities until the imperatives of adolescence led them to strike out for independence and self-sufficiency.

Today, however, with children's inclusion in the adult world both through the instrument of television and as a result of a deliberately preparatory, integrative style of child rearing, the old forms of play no longer seem to provide children with enough excitement and stimulation. What then are these so-called children to do for fulfillment if their desire to play has been vitiated and yet their entry into the working world of adulthood must be delayed for many years? The answer is precisely to get involved in those areas that cause contemporary parents so much distress: addictive television viewing during the school years followed, in adolescence or even before, by a search for similar oblivion via alcohol and drugs; exploration of the world of sensuality and sexuality before achieving the emotional maturity necessary for altruistic relationships.

Psychiatrists have observed among children in recent years a marked increase in the occurrence of depression, a state long considered antithetical to the nature of childhood. Perhaps this phenomenon is at least somewhat connected with the current sense of uselessness and alienation that children feel, a sense that play may once upon a time have kept in abeyance.

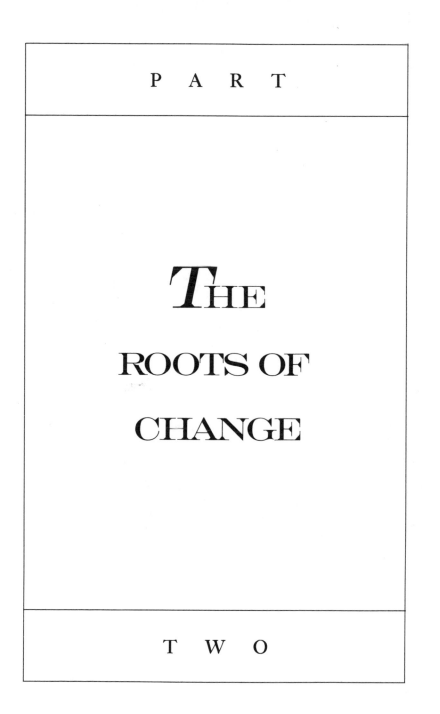

PART

THE

ROOTS OF

CHANGE

TWO

CHILDHOOD OF THE PAST

BEFORE CHILDHOOD

As we grieve for the disappearance of childhood, it is important to remember that the childlike child has not always existed. Children's new integration into adult society signals the return to a conception of childhood that existed centuries ago. As historian Philippe Ariès has pointed out in his influential study *Centuries of Childhood*,[1] the notion of childhood as a separate and special age of life came to be universally accepted only during the last two centuries. Before that, during the Middle Ages and into the seventeenth century, and sometimes, in underdeveloped areas, well into the eighteenth and even the nineteenth centuries, children were not considered to be creatures significantly different from adults. Rather, they were universally treated as smaller and somewhat inferior versions of adults.

Of course, there has always been a period of life known as infancy or early childhood when the human organism requires protective nurture. And of course very small children in medieval times were not let loose to fend for themselves (though great numbers of them perished early in life as a result of accidents, disease, or faulty nutrition). Infants *were* considered different from the rest of the population, and their difference was marked not only by special care and feeding but by special clothing, special cradles and cribs to sleep in, and even a few rudimentary playthings especially designed for their amusement. But after the age of six or seven the helpless stage was over. Now children were believed to have reached the "age of reason," and from then on they were expected to take their place in the hurly-burly of medieval society, to work and play alongside adults.

Thenceforth, there were no physical separations to mark off children from adults—no special clothes or books or toys, no special manners, no special age-graded schools where children were segregated for any part of their day.

It is hard to think of seven- or eight-year-olds today working gainfully at adult jobs, marching off with little briefcases to their offices or workshops. We can more easily understand children's inclusion in the work world of centuries past when we remember that work in those pre-industrial days often consisted of the very arts and crafts that progressive schools and camps offer today for children's amusement: spinning, weaving, basketry, candlemaking—all activities once performed at home with the help of child labor, all available today in special kits from Childcraft or Creative Playthings. Agricultural work as well—planting, working the soil, or gathering—another great occupation for children in medieval times, seems similarly attractive to children today, at least so long as it takes the form of voluntary projects labeled "science experiments" rather than enforced work.

The pastimes that filled leisure time in the medieval era were similarly suited for sharing with children. Evidence from old paintings and writings shows that many of the traditional games today reserved entirely for children—tag or hide-and-seek or blindman's bluff—were once enjoyed by large numbers of adults as well. Indoors, adults sang songs and told stories for amusement. Some of the very tales later collected by the brothers Grimm were once thought appropriate for a mixed group of children and adults. We have grown so accustomed to thinking of Grimm's fairy tales as children's stories that we rarely stop to wonder at how adult the subject matter of most of them really is. These are tales of sexual love, marriage, jealousy, and political power; it is largely the elements of fantasy and transformation that make them interesting to children.

It is likely that adults themselves in those days were more childlike, in our modern meaning of the word—that is, simpler in their ways of thinking and functioning—than they came to be in later, more complex societies. They were undoubtedly more childlike too in the sense of being more spontaneous, less self-conscious, in their behavior. As we learn in Le Roy Ladurie's book *Montaillou*,[2] a detailed picture of fourteenth-century daily life, the men and women who lived six centuries ago possessed far simpler concepts of time and space and of history than we find among adults today. They seem to have manifested a greater emotional simplicity as well, as shown by a readiness to laugh and cry in the course of everyday events. We find evidence of this more childlike quality among the adults of ancient times we meet in such works as Homer's *Odyssey*, where seasoned warriors frequently burst into tears of happiness or anguish with no self-consciousness. In anthropological studies of primitive societies we frequently discover similar "childlike" traits. (These must, of course, be distinguished from "immature" traits, being childlike only inasmuch as they resemble behavior we have come, in recent times, to associate especially with children.)

Just as we find adults seeming to be more childlike in medieval times, so we perceive that children were in some ways *less* childlike in those days than they appeared to be in more recent times, at least in their lack of innocence about adult life and particularly about adult sexuality. Until recently this innocence has been virtually synonymous with childhood. But in those long-ago days when children were thoroughly integrated into adult life, there was little chance of sheltering them from the knowledge of sexuality or of those subjects that later came to be considered unsuitable for those of "tender years": suffering, injustice, deceit, sorrow, death. How could children be kept innocent when domestic arrangements often involved an entire family sharing a large communal bed, or at least a single sleeping room? Privacy, in our sense of the word, was a concept that hardly existed in medieval society; the facts of life and death were difficult to hide from any member of the household. Besides, it never occurred to anyone that such matters *ought* to be hidden from children.

MANNERS AND SEX

When we consider the characteristic behavioral differences between children and adults in the modern era, we realize that to a great degree it is the manners adults have acquired that distinguish their behavior from children's. Untrained children of six or seven or eight cannot exhibit the same social niceties that even the most casual adults easily observe in public. Children naturally eat more piggishly, blurt out inappropriate observations ("Why are you so fat? What is that big thing on your nose?"), talk about their primitive needs in public ("Mommy, I have to go to the bathroom real bad"), and the like.

As Norbert Elias has pointed out in his history of manners, *The Civilizing Process,* it was not until recent centuries that adult standards of behavior required more restraint and control than children could manage without a good deal of training. During the Middle Ages, we understand, there was far less emphasis on manners and the public repression of instinctive drives than in later centuries. Those were times when adults customarily ate with their fingers, wiped their noses on their sleeves, belched and farted whenever they wished, urinated in public, and in general behaved much the way young children would behave today if they were not taught better. If civilization resides in those manners and repressions and controls, as some suggest, then there was simply less of it in the twelfth, thirteenth, and fourteenth centuries, among adults as well as children.

Evidence of the absence of "civilized" behavior in the Middle Ages may be seen in the books of manners that began to appear in the fifteenth, sixteenth, and seventeenth centuries. These included such admonitions as "Do not touch yourself under your clothes with your bare hands" or "It is impolite to greet someone who is urinating or defecating" or "Let no one, whoever he may be, at or after meals, early or late, foul the staircases, corridors, or closets with urine or other filth," or "Let not thy privy members be layd open to be view'd." Such instructions would not seem to us inappropriate, in some form, to offer young children. But these books were addressed to *adults,* making it clear that until that time society had sanctioned "doing what comes naturally" for all. The need to change that natural and "unmannerly" behavior of children into the ever more refined and repressed behavior of the adult world soon led to a steady and rigorous program of training during childhood. Before children acquire these manners, therefore, their behavior is noticeably different from adults', and this difference helps define them as children. As

Elias observed, children "have in the space of a few years to attain the advanced level of shame and revulsion that has developed over many centuries. Their instinctual life must be rapidly subjected to the strict control and specific molding that gives our societies their stamp, and which developed slowly over many centuries."[3]

For this reason, in medieval times, before a rigid code of manners existed for adults, the disparity between adult and child was noticeably smaller than it came to be in later times when children spent their childhood learning how to behave "properly."

It may have been the absence of courtly manners that allowed people in the Middle Ages to be more open and unrepressed about sexual matters than in the eras that followed. The idea of strictly concealing sexual drives or sexual relations seems to have been as alien to the medieval consciousness as the need to suppress a belch. But once sexuality was removed from the public sector and its concealment became an important part of everyday behavior, it was necessary, in order to avoid public embarrassment, to isolate children completely from any knowledge of adult sexuality. Only thus could parents make certain that children did not, in their impetuosity or imprudence, violate society's increasingly rigid codes about sexual secrecy. In the process of being preserved in a state of total sexual ignorance, children came to differ truly from adults in this one great area. They had, of course, always differed from adults in their reproductive capacity. Now an entire new separation between those two stages of life had been created: adults were knowledgeable (to some degree, at least) about sex and were creatures with sexual needs; children were innocent of the sexual side of life and were believed to have no sexual drives at all.

It takes an act of imagination today to conceive of a society that truly does not see children as being qualitatively different from adults. Yet how else can we explain the strange distortion of children in medieval paintings and drawings? Again and again we find artists of that period, while capturing with perfect verisimilitude the accurate proportions of the human adult form, neglecting to observe the characteristic proportions that make children in real life look not merely smaller but essentially *different* from adults: the child's outsized head in proportion to its body, the extra-large eyes, the short and rounded limbs. To be discussed further in the final section of this book, these physiological characteristics that differentiate children from adults have been called *neotenic traits* by contemporary etholo-gist Konrad Lorenz, who suggests that they serve a particular evolu-tionary function in that they trigger protective behavior towards children from adults. It is therefore significant to note their seem-ingly deliberate omission, perhaps even suppression, from the medie-val consciousness during an era when children were integrated into the adult world rather than protected from it.

A   R A D I C A L   T R A N S F O R M A T I O N

By the end of the eighteenth century a radical transformation of human relations had come to pass, one that might truly be called a Copernican revolution in thinking about children and childhood. After centuries of indifference to those needs of children that distin-guish them from adults—indeed, of unawareness that children even *had* such needs—society began to take a new interest in childhood's special qualities. "Love childhood," wrote Jean-Jacques Rousseau in 1762 in *Emile*, his treatise on education. "Indulge its games, its pleas-ures, and its lovable nature. Who has not looked back with regret on an age when laughter is always on the lip and when the spirit is always at peace. Why take away from these little innocents the pleasure of a time so short which ever escapes them?" What a contrast this attitude makes to the thinking of the era that preceded it, when children had no separate games or pleasures, and when adults might more likely breathe a sigh of relief that childhood, that stage of life when they had been lowly and inferior members of an adult-oriented society, was finally over and they were at less of a disadvantage in their daily work and play life.

As the classical spirit of the seventeenth and eighteenth centuries, with its emphasis on reason, was replaced by a great surge of Roman-ticism, children came to be appreciated in a new way. No longer seen as inferior versions of more rational adults, they came to be idealized for what were now considered their own special attributes: imagina-tion, purity, innocence, trustfulness, unselfconsciousness, and a closeness to nature that adults could only struggle to approximate. By the nineteenth century, Rousseau's nostalgia for childhood had been succeeded by a virtual worship of the child and a conviction that childhood is superior to all stages of life that follow. Wordsworth's well-known "Intimations" ode sums up the new Romantic view of childhood that saw the rest of life as a diminishment. "Heaven lies about us in our infancy!" says the poet, but "Shades of the prison-house begin to close upon the growing Boy." Accurately observing the universal tendency of children to want to grow up as fast as they can, Wordsworth exclaims: "Thou little Child, yet glorious in the might/Of heaven-born freedom on thy being's height,/Why with such earnest pains dost thou provoke/The years to bring the inevitable yoke,/Thus blindly with thy blessedness at strife?" No medieval poet would have exhorted children to delay their struggles towards adulthood. The society of that time would have considered such an idea quite daft.

Consider the image of childhood that emerges in the following passage by Lewis Carroll, that noted idolator of childhood innocence, referring to the original inspiration of his Wonderland tale, Alice Liddell: "Where were thou, dream Alice, in thy foster father's eyes? How shall he picture thee? Loving first, loving and gentle . . . then trustful, ready to accept the wildest impossibilities with all the utter trust that only dreamers know; and lastly curious, wildly curious, and with the eager enjoyment of life that comes only in the happy chorus of childhood, when all is new and fair, and when Sin and Sorrow are but names—empty words signifying nothing!"

How different a child is pictured here from the lusty little homunculus we find in medieval pictures and letters! And yet we have good reason to believe, from memoirs and reminiscences and even photographs, that children in the Victorian and Edwardian eras truly were trusting and loving and gentle and curious, truly did seem to eagerly enjoy life. The changes in childhood behavior between the two eras were direct consequences of a new attitude of protectiveness and careful nurture of children that had begun to inform child rearing in this era. For along with the Romantic concept of childhood as a time of essential purity and goodness went the practical efforts to preserve this purity and goodness by quarantining children from those corrupting influences of the adult world that might tarnish their natural splendor. Subsequently, as the child was isolated from the adult world and protected from all adult influences, he truly grew to resemble that idealized and sentimentalized image. Only in the rarefied atmosphere that came to surround children after the eighteenth century did they change from those blasphemous little versions of adults produced by the Middle Ages into those blessed little creatures apotheosized by Carroll. Then, as children presented themselves to adults in their tender, trusting, *special* ways, adults treated them more carefully, more protectively than ever before.

What brought about this great change in attitude towards children and childhood? One way to understand it is to recognize that the old integrative, nondifferentiating way of dealing with children prepared them best for the life they had to lead in feudal economies, while the new separatist, protective attitude that set in during the eighteenth century and reached its apotheosis in the nineteenth molded children into behavior patterns that a pre-industrial and industrial economy required. In an increasingly complex society it was no longer possible for children simply to melt into the adult world and function as somewhat inferior but nevertheless useful versions of adults. This had worked in past centuries, when children served as agricultural helpers or as workers in cottage industries or as apprentices to craftsmen. In such an economy the attributes required to carry out their assigned tasks successfully were persistence, perseverance, courage, and independence, virtues more readily acquired if a child is set loose early from intimate ties with those who nurtured him in infancy. Moreover, these are traits that somehow do not seem alien to the natural spirit of childhood. We can observe quite young and untrained children persisting and persevering in their natural childish pursuits— in their play, in their efforts to have their desires gratified as quickly as possible. We see, often with sinking hearts, children behaving with the most awesome courage and independence, sometimes dangling out of fifth-floor windows on a "dare," though we tend to attribute such behavior to inexperience and consider such children foolhardy rather than brave. In the individualistic agricultural and small-craft work world of bygone times, children could serve as helpers without much training and be rewarded for their natural spunk and independence. But the roles that children would have to take up eventually in an increasingly urbanized and bureaucratized society required new kinds of skills, skills that might be acquired only through the steady refinements of a lengthy education. Not only did children now need to acquire knowledge in intellectual spheres, reading and mathematical computing, but they had to learn new behavior patterns as well. These did not come naturally to a child's temperament. Slowly and painfully, children were helped to acquire such graces as cooperation, tactfulness, and social sensitivity, skills they would need someday in the new kinds of work available to adults in towns and cities.

Moreover, because of the reduced need for child labor in a complex economy, children were no longer required to work from an early age (at least not the children of the middle classes). Instead, they spent more and more of their time in age-segregated schools, away from adults and in the company of children their own age. Protected now from adult realities, both by dint of their actual separation from adult society during most of their waking hours and as a result of a deliberate decision to keep them innocent, children actually began to seem more childlike in their behavior—though perhaps only in contrast with their more sophisticated and complex elders. (Adults in the medieval era might have seemed similarly childlike had they been contrasted with their peers of later times.)

The new solicitude towards children that replaced the past's careless approach may also be explained by the appearance and gradual acceptance of the concept of developmental psychology that had its roots in the writings of Locke in the seventeenth and Rousseau in the eighteenth centuries, and came into prominence in the nineteenth century with the work of John Dewey. For the first time, as children were studied and observed and compared with adults, adults began to accept the importance of childhood as a stage of life in its relation to adulthood. They began to understand that what happens to a person as a child has a direct impact upon his adult outcome. Now parents saw that the way they brought up their children, the choices they made in their child-rearing methods (whether to breast-feed or bottle-feed, whether to spank or not, whether to be strict or lenient), had specific and possibly unalterable consequences.

NEW-ERA CHILD REARING

An important milestone on the road back to the integration of children into adult society was Freud's theory of childhood sexuality, and especially the Oedipus complex. Today the assumption of a baby love affair between a toddler and its parent of the opposite sex is rarely challenged; it is practically accepted as a scientific fact. But when Freud first formulated the idea that a little boy of three or four might have real sexual longings for his mother, it was greeted with disbelief. A society that idealized and romanticized children as little innocents could hardly help but be stunned by so radically different a view of childhood.

As a new understanding of child development showed small children to be nothing like those glorified, joyful cherubs of nineteenth-century song and story, parents began to accept the fact that children feel jealousy and rage, not only love and angelic cheer. But in embracing Freud's model, society bought far more than a new picture of a more complicated child. Unknowingly it laid the foundations for the end of childhood itself as a special stage of life. For in Freud's view, children and adults are governed by similar strong passions. In his Oedipal desires, the child differs from the adult largely in his capacity to carry out his wish; the essence of his sexuality is similar to the adult's. In the child's rages and jealousies the proposed difference is quantitative, not qualitative.

Freud's most faithful interpreter, his daughter Anna Freud, anticipated the shocked reaction of her audience of teachers to this newly undifferentiated view of childhood when she told them: "You think I have everywhere interpreted the emotions and acts of little children by analogy with the corresponding manifestations of adults, and that I describe childish behavior in language generally used only for the behavior of adults. Thus I have converted the ordinary friction of the child with his brothers and sisters into serious death wishes; and the quite innocent and tender relation of the boy to his mother into the love of a man who desires a woman sexually."[1] And indeed, she continued, that *is* what underlies children's behavior.

Freud's ideas have had such a deep influence on all contemporary thought about children that it has come to seem inevitable that some of the same emotional standards be applied to children as to adults. And yet his undifferentiated view of childhood may not be incontrovertible.

This is not to take issue with Freud's discoveries about the workings of the human heart and mind, especially those revealing the powerful influence of the unconscious on men's and women's behavior—surely an amazing contribution to scientific knowledge. Nor can one deny the grave connection he uncovered between infant and childhood experiences and later-life personality distortions. But underlying his insights is a fatalistic assumption of an essential identity between children and adults that allows their behavior to be interpreted according to the same standards. There *is* room for disagreement that such an identity exists. For one thing, the physiological differences, especially in brain chemistry, between children and adults suggest that certain similar behaviors may arise for different reasons and may have a very different significance.

As Erich Fromm[2] has pointed out in a respectful criticism of Freud, there is another way of looking at the child's so-called Oedipal passions that presupposes a greater distinction between children's and adults' ways of functioning. The child's desperate attachment to his mother may not be based on real sexual desire at all, Fromm suggests, though that is what such an attachment would spell if it were exhibited by an adult. Rather, the child's desire for his mother's exclusive attention may reveal, not a longing for sexual union, but a juvenile yearning for that blissful state of total security that she provided during the early stages of life. Moreover, that common declaration of early childhood which Freud brings up as evidence for the Oedipal conflict, "When Daddy dies I will marry you, Mommy," can only be interpreted as representing murderous rage and lust, Fromm contends, if one ignores the real differences that exist between a child and an adult. In fact, he reminds us, the four-year-old boy has little idea of what death means; he only wants his father to be away so he can have his mother to himself. From Fromm's sensible vantage point the idea of a sexual relationship, or even the desire for one, between a four-year-old and a mature woman seems far-fetched.

Nothing had been more effective in separating children from adults than the concept of childhood innocence and childhood asexuality. With the Oedipus complex Freud shattered that image and brought childhood and adulthood closer together than they had been for centuries. In a certain sense, his theory restored the child once again to its medieval position as a miniature adult.

THE PARENT AS PSYCHOANALYST

There was a time when parents confidently believed that as long as they fed their children properly, kept them out of harm's way, and gave them the proper advantages, they would grow up well. In those days the parent's major task was to train and socialize, to teach their children to conform to the requirements of the society they were born into.

As the Freudian view of childhood began to filter down from the small circle of specialists and patients of the 1920s and 1930s into the universal consciousness of parents in all classes of society, parental confidence began to evaporate. Suddenly parents were burdened with the fearful knowledge that only they stood between their child's growing up "normal" and his growing up to be a neurotic, screwed-up adult. A single false step, a traumatic experience, an inadvertent peek at the "primal scene," might cause their child to develop insomnia, impotence, or an irrational fear of horses many years later. The very fact that between the trauma and the consequent neurosis could lie a seemingly normal childhood made the situation all the more unnerving. Like those long-incubating viruses that produce minor symptoms when they first enter the body and twenty years later result in multiple sclerosis, so parental miscalculations, missteps, misunderstandings, and mistakes might lead, after a long hiatus, to the most untoward consequences. This new knowledge, when it finally penetrated, helped to facilitate the widespread adoption by the end of the 1960s of a new child-rearing style, one no longer focused on the child's socialization but on its mental health.

To suggest that a new element entered parent-child relations during the last generation is not to say that parents did not use psychology in their child-rearing strategies before 1970. After all, as long ago as the twenties and thirties parents had begun to temper their child care with a new understanding of child development and child psychology, much of it based on Freud's theories. Indeed, by the 1950s, the repressive ways that had characterized child rearing of Freud's day were pretty much a thing of the past, and a psychologically based, "permissive" approach had taken over.

But the "permissive" style of child rearing of the fifties, though informed by Freud's ideas, continued to operate according to the old principle of parent-as-socializer, child-as-trainee, that went back to Freud's own day. Indeed, when the permissive practices of the fifties and sixties are compared with the truly new parental style that followed, it is evident that a distinct if modified authoritarian spirit still dominated the Spock-marked parents of that era. While parents of the 1940s and 1950s were undoubtedly far more psychologically shrewd than parents of earlier times (which caused them to permit certain child behavior that parents before them had suppressed), in reality they, not the child, continued to make all the child-rearing decisions. The permissive parent said, "Danny won't eat his spinach because he is in a stage when children don't like anything new. Let's try spinach again next year and permit him to stick to peas for now." The more old-fashioned parent might have said, "Danny won't eat his spinach because he's a bad boy, and therefore he must be punished." But in each case the parent was in control, making decisions about the child's life based on firm beliefs and principles.

The new child-rearing approach that set in by the 1970s, one that might well be called a "psychoanalytic" style, presupposes a different, far more collaborative relationship between parent and child. No longer does the parent operate from his vantage point of superior knowledge, of *adult* convictions. Rather, the child is enlisted as an accomplice in his own upbringing. At every step along the way the parent tries to discover why the child is behaving as he is behaving, why he, the parent, is reacting as he is reacting. And when the child misbehaves, the parents do not use "child psychology" to bring him around to more socially acceptable behavior. Instead they try to make him *understand* why he feels the way he does by providing the sort of enlightenment a therapist might give a patient. In a sense, the parent becomes the child's psychoanalyst.

It was the sociologist Talcott Parsons[3] who first compared the doctor's role in psychotherapy to the parent's role in child rearing, suggesting certain similarities between mental illness and the child's family status. The child, Parsons argued, cannot function in adult society independently, just as the mentally ill person cannot. The success of psychotherapy, he explained, springs from this subterranean identification between the condition of childhood and the condition of mental illness. By the same token (though Parsons never continued in this direction), child rearing may be seen as a "cure" for the aberrant condition of childhood. This therapeutic view of parenthood has become, in varying degrees, a common phenomenon today.

"As far as I'm concerned," a Bedford, New York father of three children asserts, "the great difference between growing up in my generation and my children's generation isn't television or the sexual revolution. It is Sigmund Freud's legacy. The fact of the matter is that my wife and I articulate all our concerns to the children in a very deliberate, psychological way. It's as if our family were one big group-therapy session. Sometimes we're so self-conscious about it all that we spend as much time talking to the kids about what we've done with them as we actually spend doing things with them."

Another parent, a mother of two children, describes a similar approach: "Half the time we talk to the kids, we're practically psychoanalyzing them—and ourselves. And we've been doing this kind of thing with them from their earliest years, explaining their feelings back to them, trying to let them in on why we do things."

One has only to listen to the particular tone of so many parents today who negotiate with their children, even preschoolers, in an almost conspiratorial manner to recognize that a very different parental attitude towards children has set in. As one follows the tireless

69714

explaining, even pleading, not for the child to give in, but for him to *understand,* that has become a natural part of so many parents' *modus operandi,* it becomes apparent that this is not exactly the way parents, even progressive ones, spoke to their children ten or fifteen years ago. To be sure, the good parent of the fifties or sixties also spent considerable time patiently explaining things to his child. But it was the ways of the world the parent clarified—the world of nature, of politics, of social relations. He answered his child's questions seriously and without condescension, just as the child experts advocated (a step in the direction of nondifferentiation between adult and child), and spoke in whole sentences, eschewing baby-talk. Indeed, from the substance of his words to the child he might have been conversing with another adult. But in reality the parent was pretending! He was always aware that this was something *good* for the child, something that would make the child feel "grown up" (even if he was only four), that might even help him develop "skills in the language arts." The parent was always aware of the gap between the child and himself.

But a great many of today's laborious parental explanations refer, not to the way things work or the causality of natural phenomena, but to the parent's own feelings and motivations, anxieties, insecurities, and to the possible meanings of the interactions between himself and the child from the psychological point of view. Everywhere today parents are explicating the texts of themselves, trying to get their children to understand, to agree, to forgive, instead of simply telling the kids what to do. Now the parent is no longer pretending; the child has really come to seem a psychological equal.

THE MAGIC YEARS

Parents did not have to go into psychoanalysis themselves in order to be deeply influenced in their child rearing by that discipline's presuppositions about human behavior.

The spread of the so-called psychoanalytic child-rearing style received a boost from the publication in 1959 of a highly influential child-rearing book based on psychoanalytic principles: *The Magic Years,* by Selma Fraiberg. Just as Betty Friedan's book *The Feminine*

Mystique raised women's consciousness precisely at that historical moment when a great number of socially mutagenic agents had simultaneously converged, so Fraiberg's book appeared at the onset of a great period of change for the American family. It fell upon the receptive ears of parents of the 1960s who were looking for a new kind of child rearing, and remains influential to this day.*

A comparison of Fraiberg's ideas with those of that other successful child guru of the era, Dr. Benjamin Spock, helps to illuminate the difference between old-style psychological child rearing and the less authoritative psychoanalytic style that has replaced it today. It may be seen that a very different conception of childhood and adulthood underlies each one.

Spock's famous child-care manual was subtended by a simple but crucial presumption: sharp boundaries exist between children and adults. Parents are adult, children are children, and different rules apply to each group. Spock's very title, *The Common Sense Book of Baby and Child Care*, emphasized the adultness of the audience being addressed, adults having among their natural gifts enough common sense to deal successfully with those less sensible creatures, children. The first words of the book, "You know more than you think you do," stressed parental capability and established Spock's basic premise: that parents, in their ability to nurture, to protect, to use strategies of one sort or another, are a breed apart from children. From beginning to end the book exuded confidence in parents' good instincts and basic ability to deal with the job at hand—raising children successfully. It is interesting to note that when a revised edition of the book was published in 1968, the words "common sense" had been excised from the title, making it simply *Baby and Child Care*. It is as if the very notion of common sense had now become alien to a new consciousness abroad in the land.

The title of Fraiberg's book, *The Magic Years*, carried less reassuring overtones, implying that there is something beyond a parent's control, something irrational, weird, indeed "magic," about a child's development. The book might well have begun like this: "You know *less* than

---

*According to Fraiberg's publisher, Charles Scribner's Sons, more than three-quarters of a million copies of *The Magic Years* had been sold by the end of 1982.

you think you do," and have gone on to assure the parent, "You will never get to the bottom of it. So beware." As Fraiberg went on to spell out the fatalistic principles of psychoanalytic theory as applied to practical aspects of child rearing, she introduced a new element of uncertainty into parents' minds just at a time when uncertainty was assailing them from other directions—uncertainty about their sexuality, their marriage, their government, their economic future. At this time parents began to doubt their ability to raise their children successfully. When reading *The Magic* Years, their insecurity deepened not only because Fraiberg's application of Freud to child rearing emphasized the potentially destructive effects of parental authority and power on the child's developing psyche, but because on every page the book implied a certain parity between child and adult that changed child rearing from the simple benevolent despotism it had been for centuries to a more complex, more perilous, more *democratic* process, one that many parents felt instinctively was beyond their powers to pull off successfully.

Consider the difference between Fraiberg's and Spock's opinions on that controversial child-rearing issue to spank or not to spank. Spock is quite complaisant about spanking. Short of actually promoting physical punishment, he writes:

> If an angry parent keeps himself from spanking, he may show his irritation in other ways: for instance, by nagging the child half the day, or trying to make him feel deeply guilty. I'm not particularly advocating spanking, but I think it is less poisonous than lengthy disapproval, because it clears the air, for parent and child.[4]

Spock's unquestioning assumption that the child is essentially different from the adult becomes clear if we try to extend that pro-spanking argument to *adult* human relations. We know perfectly well that pacifist Benjamin M. Spock would not advocate that a husband smartly smack a wife who has displeased him in order to "clear the air," nor would he suggest that the best way for a wife to deal with an annoying husband is with a well-placed kick. No: for adults, obviously the "lengthy disapproval" and the guilt-inflicting strategy are preferable. But different rules apply, according to Spock, in parent-child relations.

Fraiberg, in contrast to Spock, condemns spanking unequivocally.[5] Spanking is too easy, she feels, since it lets the child off with no residue of guilt. Here is how Fraiberg's argument against spanking goes:

> The experience of a sense of guilt for wrong-doing is necessary for the development of self-control. . . . guilt feelings are indispensable for the development of a conscience. . . . We need to make use of a child's guilty reactions in training for self-control. . . . If we do not hold a child responsible for his own acts, if we treat the act as if it were divorced from the person, we only provide a ready-made system for evasion of responsibility.

Fraiberg is talking about young children, it must be remembered, between the ages of three and six. We have gotten so accustomed to this sort of approach that the words sound unexceptional to us. Yet not so very long ago the use of the words "evasion of responsibility" or "development of a conscience" would have sounded laughable if applied to a child of four or five or six. The very definition of a child of that age back in, say, 1945 or even 1957 involved a carefree irresponsibility and an almost complete absence of conscience.

Fraiberg goes on to explain why spanking is wrong:

> The "lessons" which a spanking is supposed to teach somehow fail to become integrated in the form of conscience . . . the motive for controlling the naughty impulse is a motive that comes from the outside, the fear of external authority and a fear of punishment, and we find that a conscience that functions on this basis is not a very reliable conscience. If fear of punishment from the outside, instead of the child's own guilt feelings, sets off the danger signal, there are a number of subterfuges open to the child. He may only need to assure himself that he will not be found out in order to pursue his mischief. Or, calculating the pleasure-pain risks, he may decide to have his fun even if he has to pay for it later. But the child who is capable of developing guilt feelings when he considers doing

something which is "bad" has a signal system within himself which will warn him and inhibit the act. Unlike the child whose control system is "outside," this child with a conscience does not need a policeman around in order to control his behavior. The child with a conscience has his policeman inside.

But wait a moment. When you stop to think of it, this "child" Fraiberg describes above, the one with the internalized conscience, doesn't sound much like a child. In fact, he sounds suspiciously like an adult! From the adult's point of view, it is certainly preferable to live with a five-year-old who doesn't need a "policeman" around to control his behavior—who can control himself. And if, more to the point, the parent is not going to be around in any case to monitor the child's behavior, because of work or the exigencies of social life, it is less a matter of preference than of dire necessity to have a child with an internalized conscience.

Fraiberg quotes an "intelligent and conscientious mother" who once took issue with her anti-spanking argument because she didn't want to make her child feel guilty about misbehavior. The woman argued: "I think it's far better to smack a child and get it over with. Clear the air. Then everyone feels better and it's done. When I was a child I much preferred my mother's spankings to my father's disapproval. All he had to do was look at me reproachfully and I felt miserable. With Mother you were naughty, you got a swift smack, and it was all over. All of us kids preferred Mother's smacks to Dad's way."

This, of course, is exactly what Dr. Spock proposes. He even uses the same phrase, "Clear the air." The mother confirms from her own childhood experience Spock's idea that spanking is easier on a child, more merciful. Fraiberg, however, is not as concerned with mercy as with efficiency. She feels that " 'Mother's smacks' left no residue of guilt feelings, no painful feelings to deal with within oneself." She believes that the spanked child who thinks, "I was naughty, I paid for it, and now we are all square," is getting off too easily.

Yet this once seemed a perfectly fair deal for a child to make with his parents, and characterized most of the family transactions that

occurred in normal childhoods. People *expected* children to misbehave, to be naughty, to get in trouble. Part of the definition of a child
that distinguished him from a grown-up was an impulsiveness and
willingness to chance punishment in order to explore or experiment
or gratify a desire. No one doubted but that the young cutups who
stole peaches from Farmer Brown's fields, who smoked cornsilk
behind the cowbarn, who played hooky to go to the movies, who
blackmailed their older sisters when they caught them "spooning,"
would grow up into honest, conscientious citizens who would neither steal nor blackmail nor shirk on their responsibilities. Childhood
was *different.*

In *The Magic Years* Fraiberg never *recommends* that parents not be
firm and decisive, that children not be treated as children. But just
as a perfect confidence in parental common sense colors all the writings of Dr. Spock, so in Fraiberg there is a sense, as in Freud, of
complexity, of ambiguity, and of all the things that can go wrong,
not only if the parent does not *do* the right things but if he does not
feel the right things. The inadvertent impact of the book was to cause
parents to act less decisively and to cause child rearing to became a
cooperative enterprise between parent and child. Even that last parental behavior to bear to this day the old-fashioned designation of
training—toilet training—was to become, in recent times, a prolonged period of desperate parental negotiation and child obduracy,
thanks to a new awareness of the deep psychological significance of
the event and an understanding of what can go wrong if it is not
accomplished properly that Fraiberg and other psychoanalytically
oriented advisers conveyed.

These days toilet training marks the beginning of a parent-child
relationship in which the child easily senses the parent's uncertainty
and lack of confidence. The child, needless to say, has not read Freud
and hasn't a clue as to *why* his parents are so uncertain; nevertheless,
he uses it to his advantage in order to gain his own way in other stages
of socialization. "Don't throw food at the table, dear" becomes a sort
of negotiation that would have been beyond the comprehension of
old-style parents, for whom food throwing was an improper child

behavior, one that had to be quickly and inexorably nipped in the bud, a behavior, what's more, that bore no relation, in the minds of those unenlightened parents of the past, to the child's sexual development or his anal-oral compulsion, or whatever.

A TERRIBLE AUTONOMY

Rather than engaging a small child in negotiations as if he were an equal, parents of long ago believed in breaking the will early in life. In a study of Puritan child rearing in seventeenth-century America,[6] historian John Demos explored the effect of a repressive child-rearing style on a child's personality development. By studying historical documents of an era when a strict and unyielding parental style prevailed, Demos noted certain psychological characteristics of the adults of that community that seemed connected with their early experience. A similar look at recent society-wide child-rearing changes might similarly illuminate certain new psychological characteristics of today's adults and children.

Using Erik Erikson's psychoanalytic model of early childhood development,[7] Demos studied the ways the Puritans dealt with children at two crucial stages of life. The first stage, from birth to about the age of two, is the time, according to Erikson, when basic trust and security are developed for life. The second stage, between the ages of about two and five, is the period when the child must develop autonomy and a separate identity from its parents in order to gain a sense of self-esteem. While Puritan infants were offered a cozy, unrestricted mode of life during their first two years, with breast-feeding often continuing for twelve to sixteen months, and while the immediate family surroundings were generally warm and intimate and gratifying for an infant, everything changed abruptly during the child's second year. In colonial New England, just at the age when the child normally begins to express its own wishes and to explore the boundaries of its independence from its parents, a terrible test of the wills ensued. This was the classic confrontation between what the Puritans believed to be "original sin," manifest in the child's burgeoning assertiveness, and the parents' authority, representing God's will. Thus, just at the stage when, according to Erikson, the child's major task is the formation of autonomy and the consequent development of pride and self-esteem, the Puritan child was thwarted at every turn.

What was the result of such treatment? In Erikson's view, the consequence of a failure to develop autonomy at this crucial stage of life is a lasting sense of shame, guilt, doubt, and insecurity. And indeed, Demos proposes, these emotions were greatly in evidence during early colonial days. Puritans, we learn, were engaged in an endless search for forgiveness in God's eyes and suffered from a steady sense of guilt. Puritan customs such as the shaming of offenders by the use of stocks or scarlet letters point out how peculiarly vulnerable members of that society were to shame and humiliation..

Clearly, something very basic has changed in our psychological make-up. The very notion that being forced to wear a garment with some sort of shameful symbol would have the slightest impact on today's population is laughable. Why, half the world these days seem to be wearing T-shirts that proudly proclaim "I am not a virgin" or a variety of embarrassing, self-deprecating messages.

Our missing sense of shame may be explained by a look at today's child during that very stage of development when a child struggles for autonomy. While the Puritan toddler fought a battle of wills that he couldn't possibly win, today's preschooler hardly needs to lift a finger to gain victory. Not only are parents aware, through their understanding of psychology, that it would not serve the child's psychological development to impede his efforts at independence, but they realize that it wouldn't serve their own purposes either. In a society of adults struggling with personal problems—economic, social, sexual, and what have you—parents are less likely to sabotage a child's efforts to stand on his own two feet. If there is anything today's child is encouraged to achieve quickly and efficiently it is autonomy, separation from the mother, independence.

Today's children and young adults brought up according to newly permissive principles are a singularly open, unashamed, un-guilt-ridden lot. Older people these days are often taken aback at the easygoing, casual, offhand manner today's children display in their relationships with adults, be they parents, teachers, school principals, or strangers they run into (and do not give their seats up to) on the bus. Surely this conforms with Erikson's prediction that a child allowed to develop autonomy freely during early childhood will be confident and unashamed. But what adults today miss, perhaps unbeknownst to themselves, is just a little touch of that bashfulness that seemed to be part of the very definition of a child in bygone days, a result, if Erikson is right, of repressive child rearing. For the odds are that never before have children emerged from early childhood with such perfect, such perfectly terrible, autonomy.

SEVEN

THE END OF SYMBIOSIS

"Women and children first!" was once the cry as the ship went down. In the old days everyone knew that the "fair sex" as well as the "wee ones" required special care and protection.

As we consider our changed attitudes towards children in recent years, and particularly our conviction that protection no longer serves them well, it is important to examine the changes that have taken place in society's attitudes towards women, as well as women's changed ideas about themselves. For just as women and children were once lumped together automatically as a single group in need of special attention on shipboard, so, for at least two centuries, women and children's lives were inextricably bound together as a symbiotic entity. It was this amalgamation that allowed childhood to develop into a special territory, as it were, with strict boundaries separating it from the regular adult world. And unquestionably it was the severing of this symbiosis and the end of exclusivity between mothers and children, beginning in the turbulent years of the 1960s, that brought children out of their sheltered province and into the great wide world.

Before the eighteenth century, before the "modern family" as a nuclear unit came into existence, before industrialization and urbanization altered ancient work patterns by taking men away from the household or farm to distant workplaces and leaving the women to "mind the house and kids," women were as vital to the proper functioning of the economy as men. Women worked as spinners, weavers, manufacturers of a variety of domestic artifacts and foodstuffs, or as agricultural workers alongside men. Labor was specialized according to sex, as it had been from ancient times, but in many ways the sexes were interdependent economically. After infancy and early childhood, children too were trained to work according to sex, girls working in the household under the supervision of women, boys helping at jobs and learning skills that were traditionally assigned to men. There was no feeling in those days that children were the special province of mothers.

Then women lost their direct economic function. As the various articles they had once produced came to be manufactured outside the household and as their agricultural chores were taken over by men and machines, women became more and more isolated within the home. And not surprisingly, as they grew increasingly dependent on men both economically and emotionally, they came to be seen as weak and vulnerable creatures in need of protection.

An advice book for "young ladies" published in 1830 counseled that "in whatever situation of life a woman is placed from her cradle to the grave, a spirit of obedience and submission, pliability of temper and humility of mind are required from her." Another writer observed of woman in 1854: "She feels herself weak and timid. She needs a protector." Or as Grace Greenwood wrote in 1850: "True feminine genius is ever timid, doubtful, and clingingly dependent; a perpetual childhood."[1] From hardy helpmates to clinging vines, women certainly had gone a long way—though not necessarily forward.

Meanwhile, not surprisingly, children too underwent a similar metamorphosis, from expendable, relatively independent (though lowly) cogs in the feudal economic system to tender dependents, in need of care and nurture and protection.

A CRUCIAL ATTACHMENT

As women's power diminished over the years, in one area their influence increased a hundredfold: in their role as mothers. Indeed, by the turn of the century a "cult of motherhood" had sprung up, celebrating the mother-child tie and introducing the concept of a special and unique maternal love and care.

That the attachment between a child and its mother has some

special bearing on its adult outcome, an understanding so widely accepted today that it is considered beyond question, is, we are surprised to realize, a relatively modern conception. Before the revolution in thinking about children that occurred in the eighteenth century, it would have seemed preposterous to suggest that a child's early relationships might unalterably affect its development. Not that mothers did not love their children in past ages; literature from the Bible to the works of Homer and the ancient Greeks is filled with examples of maternal love for children. But the idea that there is something *crucial* about motherly love, that without it the child will fail to thrive, is absent from the general consciousness of the past. Consider, for instance, an example of maternal deprivation to be found in Shakespeare's play *The Winter's Tale*. When a new mother, Hermione, is unjustly accused of infidelity by her jealous husband, their baby, Perdita, is taken from her and exposed on a wild and deserted seacoast. As luck would have it, the infant is found by a crude but kindly shepherd and raised by him. Yet no one is particularly surprised that the girl grows up to be wise, noble, and eloquent far beyond her lowly foster parent's ability and proves to be unaffected by the traumatic experience of her early maternal deprivation. Today, we would expect such a child to grow up to be an unfeeling sociopath. In fact, the story of Perdita's infant fate reminds us of nothing so much as the Oedipus myth, in which the tragic hero begins life similarly rejected by his mother and father, exposed to the wintry elements. Again, no one in times past, not even Freud, was surprised that this abused and neglected child grew up to be a fine young man, heroic and capable of love (though not a very propitious love, to be sure) after his terrible early experiences.

As society attributed greater importance to mothers, and mothers and children became ever more closely allied, a change occurred in attitudes towards children. Children, in concept, began to lose a certain amount of the vigor, the power even, that had once accompanied their position in society—a power, in fact, that had caused them at times to be somewhat feared. Syllogistically it worked like this: if women are weak and dependent, and if women are in power over children, then children are even weaker and even more dependent than women. Indeed, if women are to be seen as helpless creatures in need of men's protection, then how much more in need of protection from the dangers of the world must children be! No wonder children became the subjects of anxious care and protective nurture the like of which had never been lavished on them before.

The growing view of the child as helpless and completely dependent on the mother for love and care conferred power on mothers, who were otherwise powerless. These mothers were aware, if only subliminally, that in their childlike position and childlike behavior towards men they were not achieving their full potential. Indeed, for women it was a source of compensatory self-esteem to be able to wield the same sort of power over their children as the menfolk held over them. This was clearly the message of another nineteenth-century writer of advice who rhapsodized to his female readers: "If in becoming a mother you reached the climax of your happiness, you have also taken a higher place in the scale of being . . . you have gained an increase in power."[2]

The romantic view of childhood as a special time of joy is not unrelated to women's former position as objects of veneration, as beings who operated under totally different laws of behavior than men. For precisely as men of the nineteenth century romanticized and idealized the special "feminine" qualities that women were said to possess—purity, spirituality, piety, instinctive modesty—so it was possible to differentiate children from adults by means of special qualities children alone possessed—imaginativeness, playfulness. And just as those "feminine" qualities caused men to treat women in special ways, so too children's endearing differences caused them to be enclosed ever more securely in the world of the home and family. Slowly, in their cozy and protected confines these two special, almost unearthly beings, women and children, merged into an inseparable unit wherein the one gained sustenance and meaning from the other. Rearing children became the foremost, the exclusive, the almost sacred occupation of women. Maternal love came to be seen as the most important ingredient of a child's early experience. A symbiosis was formed, one that was strengthened, almost cemented into an unbreakable bond, by the later writing of John Bowlby and others who emphasized the disastrous consequences of maternal deprivation on the child's emotional development.

It must be understood that this situation did not exist for all mothers and children. Only the relatively privileged classes could afford to protect and isolate women and children; older ways prevailed among the lower classes. We know well that at the very height of the cult of motherhood and sentimentalization of childhood in the nineteenth century, great numbers of needy women and children labored in factories and mills. Nevertheless, the new family model and the new attitudes towards women and children came to be increasingly prevalent, infiltrating all classes of society by the first decades of the twentieth century as protective labor laws removed children from the labor market altogether.

THE END OF PROTECTION

By the middle of the twentieth century the transformation of the family into a domestic haven was complete. Postwar prosperity and the growth of suburbia isolated women and children in what seemed a paradise of material comforts and almost pastoral safety. Home continued to be a shelter where innocent children and childlike women were protected from the dangers of the harsh world. As in the nineteenth century, society in all its social and cultural manifestations continued to maintain a protective position towards women. Men reserved strong language and racy stories for the company of their peers; cultural media—plays, books, and as the century wore on, radio and movies—adhered to standards of purity such that the delicate sensibilities of women, to say nothing of children, would not be offended. When mothers finally broke out of their protective confines—or perhaps, when mothers saw the protective confines disintegrate about them—children could no longer remain alone in the cocoon. And out they came, into the world of R-rated movies and live-in boyfriends and rape and murder and government corruption and all.

In part, it was television, impossible to control, that brought the long-hidden outside world into the lives of both women and children and caused parents to abandon some of their seemingly instinctive sheltering of children, if only to prepare them to some degree for what they were bound to see on TV anyway. And partly it was the women's liberation movement, gaining momentum in the mid-sixties and causing women to reject their roles as child-women and child-wives. With Betty Friedan's publication of *The Feminine Mystique*, the scales began to fall from American women's eyes with an almost audible clatter. Inevitably, as women began openly to object to being protected from the realities of life, being dependent, being treated as little pets, being condescended to under the guise of adoration and special care, they began to resist dealing with their own children in a similar manner. They recognized that the protective circle of secrecy and restrictiveness surrounding them was also preventing them from fully developing their strengths and abilities, and they began to wonder whether such treatment might similarly hamper their children's development.

THE NEW ASSERTIVENESS

There was a long period of time when mothers and children comfortably accepted a less than equal role in the politics of the family. But under the intoxicating and infectious influence of the women's liberation movement, women began to reject the authoritarian family setup that had once seemed so comfortable and so inevitable. The various effects of women's new assertiveness on their own lives and destinies have been often discussed. The indirect impact of their changed attitudes on the children in the family has not been given equal attention. And yet much of the "new" behavior manifested by today's children may be directly connected to this change.

When women's position in the family was unequal and this inequality was universally accepted, when women served meals to their husbands and children as a matter of course, and deferred to their husbands in all family policy decisions (while continuing to wield a subtle, indirect influence—ever the "woman's way"), mothers easily assumed the very position of authority over their children that husbands assumed over wives. It seemed a natural way to behave—

natural that those who were dependent and vulnerable should accept the authority of those who were in every way more "adult." Thus women were expected to follow the lead of their husbands, and children to obey their parents. But when women began seeking a more equal relationship with their husbands—not merely more equal in distribution of domestic labors and child care but more equal in their relations with each other—when women for the first time gained the freedom to be assertive and even aggressive towards men, it became harder for them to be quite as authoritative with the kids. Somehow, as wives became more open about their angers and resentments and as they gained the self-confidence to become less dependent emotionally upon their husbands, so they began, perhaps unconsciously at first, to encourage similar openness and independence in their children. It was as if they could not challenge a certain style of behavior in their relationships with their husbands and still demand that same behavior—subservience and deference—from their kids: it didn't seem fair.

One of the great problems that accompanied the gradual turning away from an authoritarian structure in the family (a structure that subtended the most "democratic" American families of the forties and fifties, families which, in spite of their child-centered approaches, nevertheless always maintained a clear-cut notion of who were the parents and who were the kids—who, in short, was "in charge") was the uneasiness and tension that arises when parents adopt a deliberately new child-rearing style. The children's new assertiveness, allowed if not encouraged by a new, less repressive parent-child relationship, conflicted with the parents' deep-rooted preconceptions of how children *ought* to behave. For while mothers began purposefully to bring up their children less repressively than they themselves had been reared, encouraging them to express their feelings openly just as the parents were learning to do in their own therapy sessions and consciousness-raising groups, they nevertheless could not suppress their unhappiness about some of the behavior that their new style of child rearing was encouraging in their children: rudeness, disrespectfulness, open anger, whiny irritability, defiance. When the six-year-old who has been asked to go to bed or clear the dinner table looks his parents in the eye and says, "No, I won't and you can't make me!" the parents come to understand that they are involved in a different sort of relationship than they had with their parents in years past.

In addition to new child-rearing styles, changing relations between husbands and wives in the 1970s and 1980s had a direct bearing on children's behavior. The old style of marital relationship most couples today find unacceptable—the well-defined, hierarchical, male-dominated arrangement—required the mother to repress her feelings, to hold back some resentments, in exchange for an orderly, stable, workable family life; this could not help but require a similar emotional cautiousness from the children. In such a family it was as unthinkable for a child to scream, "I hate you, you mean old pig!" at his mother as it would have been for the mother to tell the child about her sexual dissatisfactions in marriage. The impulses that led parents to hide feelings and realities from each other quite naturally led to a somewhat secretive manner towards the children. Above all, husbands maintained an unworldly, protected refuge for both women and children of the family. Men who might be ruthless in the business world, doctors who might face violence and pain in their daily practice, lawyers who might be engaged in morally question-able contests of law, men who daily experienced unfairness, cruelty, and bitter competition in their work lives, returned home each night to a world where their wives and children had been sequestered in almost haremlike seclusion. In this atmosphere wives and children, in an unwritten but inflexible *quid pro quo,* maintained the home as a refuge for their menfolk: women, by being "supportive" (to use a word that acquired such new meanings in the very different family relationship that was to follow in the 1970s and 1980s), submissive, and domesticated—child-wives in many ways; children, by being inno-cent, "childlike," and respectful. It is not hard to see that when home ceased to be a protected haven—thanks to the inroads of television, the consequences of divorce, the exigencies of two-career families— children could no longer keep their part of the bargain: the natural, innocent, bashful, reticent, trusting child of the past was replaced by the savvy, cool, self-protective, remarkably open and assertive model of today.

T H E   C H I L D - W I F E

There is a parallel, as we have seen, between the posture of innocence and vulnerability women formerly maintained and the innocent, childlike demeanor children once presented to the world; each served a particular function. As both women and children began to adopt more worldly and assertive ways, women's relations with their husbands and children's relations with their parents were affected in parallel ways.

Many of the popular movies of the forties and fifties illustrated society's former view of women as childlike creatures. Take as an example that old-time Hollywood classic of the romantic genre, *Rebecca.* Laurence Olivier, playing Maxim de Winter, the worldly, experienced hero, marries Joan Fontaine, the nameless heroine, for the contrast she presents to his wicked, sexually depraved first wife, Rebecca, now dead. Fontaine as child-woman is the very antithesis of Rebecca. "It's a pity you have to grow up," Olivier murmurs to Fontaine during their brief courtship, adding, "Please don't ever be thirty-seven years old." After their marriage her role, now as child-wife, remains the same. As Olivier helps Fontaine on with a sweater, he answers her plaintive question "Do I *have* to put it on?" with an answer that defines their relationship: "Certainly. You can't be too careful with children." The child-wife, we see, is protected in her innocence and helplessness. When an intimidating relative's visit is imminent, Olivier assures his bride: "Don't worry, I'll be back in time to protect you." It is apparent that the new mistress of Manderley, Olivier's imposing estate, is not a *real* adult; whenever she encounters one of *that* species, any independent, assertive, capable grown-up, she turns into a cringing and submissive creature filled with fear that she might do something wrong, something unseemly.

The advantages of a child-wife to Maxim de Winter are apparent and symbolize the similar advantages the child-wife offers husbands in real life. The husband of a child-wife doesn't face the threat of his wife's sexual misbehavior; children, after all, are relatively sexless— or at least they seemed to be in those days. In this movie Joan Fontaine is portrayed in a singularly unerotic way, in her prim little skirts and blouses, her knee socks and cardigans. Instead of sexual adventures, the child-wife devotes herself to household duties, flower arranging, care of her husband, and soon enough, to the care of her children, her most natural future allies in the family. Never would she have to fear them!

Power rather than partnership is the husband's share when married to a child-wife, while the wife's part of the bargain is protection, a buffer against the cold, hard world that the husband must deal with daily, protection that will similarly enclose the children someday.

Finally, as husband of a child-wife, Maxim de Winter enjoys that superior self-satisfaction that comes from protecting the helpless and from watching, from a higher level, the "cute" ways and antics of the young. When the movie reaches its climax and the child-wife is forced to grow up and learn a terrible truth about her husband's past, De Winter's strongest feeling is not relief or happiness that he has another adult to share his burdens; it is regret. He looks at her sadly and says, "It's gone forever, that funny, young, lost look. In a few hours you've grown so much older!" In fact, his regret is not unlike that parents often feel when their children grow up and assert them-selves, preparing to fly from the nest. Though parents *should* be happy at signs of burgeoning self-sufficiency in their children—after all, raising capable adults has always been the main purpose of child rearing—they inevitably feel a certain sense of loss. Their children's dependence was gratifying: it made the parents feel good.

What happened when the American woman abandoned the pedes-tal and dropped the child-woman guise? (And much of it *was* a guise, as witnessed by scores of 1950s magazine articles advising girls and women to *pretend* to be dumber than their boyfriends.) Among the many other consequences of women's struggle for greater equality within marriage was the end of that gratification that husbands had once derived from protecting their wives. In a study of marital infi-delity, a husband who is having an affair tells of his feelings towards his inamorata: "I love the protectiveness I feel towards her when she is sleeping in my arms." When asked what attributes he valued in his rejected wife, he answered, "Her stability, strength, intelligence, and efficiency." All these are adult characteristics, while protectiveness is felt towards someone more vulnerable than oneself. This is not to suggest that only if a woman retains a childlike demeanor in a marriage will her husband remain faithful. Rather, it points out the particular gratifications that the child-woman affords the male ego, and the possible difficulties that two equal adults might face in maintaining a permanent, long-term relationship. When one considers the conflicts, tensions, and strains that descend on a family when a teenager begins to assert his or her autonomy and independence, and compares it with the more stable and peaceful, though unequal, configuration of a family with young children, one begins to understand the difficulties the contemporary family faced when the child-woman began to grow up.

WORKING WOMEN

Though by the middle of the twentieth century the child-woman had come a long way from the nineteenth-century model of an infantilized, timid, fearful clinging vine of a female, and though the 1940s and 1950s abounded in the rhetoric of equality within marriage and partnership between husband and wife, nevertheless, so long as the family pattern remained breadwinner-husband and stay-at-home wife, women continued to be sheltered and unequal. And so, understandably, did the children. In spite of higher education levels, diversified interests, and their proven capacity for "men's work" (Rosie the Riveter, for example, during World War II), women continued to be treated more like children than adults. Since they were entirely dependent on their husbands economically, they had a lot at stake in making their marriages work, happy or not; they didn't know how to survive outside marriage, and even if they wanted to try, their opportunities for an independent existence were limited.

In a single generation a remarkable and unprecedentedly swift change occurred in women's working patterns, brought about partly through the imperatives of women's liberation and partly through the imperatives of economic need. According to a recent Census Bureau report,[3] the percentage of married women with children under eighteen who were in the labor force grew from 18 percent in 1950 to 54 percent in 1980. There was an even more dramatic leap in outside employment among women with children of preschool age, whose participation in the labor market almost quadrupled, going from 12 percent in 1950 to 45 percent in 1980. By the end of the 1970s, work had become the rule rather than the exception for American mothers.

Of course, in a sharply declining economy, a great many women joined the work force, not to seek liberation and equality, but out of sheer economic necessity. But whether they worked out of choice or need, their own human lot frequently improved when they left domesticity. A 1978 study, for instance, concluded that women who work outside the house enjoy greater self-esteem and suffer less anxiety than women who mind the house and kids. Similarly, a National Institutes of Health survey of 2,300 Chicago adults suggested that good jobs serve as a sort of preventive medicine for women: while the researchers discovered that women as a group suffered twice as many psychiatric symptoms as men, among women with high-status jobs the symptoms were as infrequently encountered as among the men surveyed.

It is hardly surprising, in the face of women's improved condition, that work has become a central and valued part of women's lives in the last twenty years. But what about the children who are no longer the primary concern of housebound mothers? Has their mothers' greater self-esteem and contentment led to benefits for them?

Certainly, all things being equal, children would be better off with a cheerful, confident mother than with a depressed, anxious drudge. But all things are not really equal these days. As women are no longer willing to sacrifice their own well-being and take an unfair share of the burdens of child care, too often no one at all steps in to take full charge of the children. While they may not be left to starve or wander naked through the streets, nevertheless they are likely to receive less care and supervision than they enjoyed with a stay-at-home mother, wretched and unhappy though she may have been. Such children are more likely, in today's social and cultural environment, to infiltrate adult life and find themselves partaking of adult experiences that they are developmentally unprepared to deal with. While they may survive, they are less likely than their more protected counterparts to attain their optimal emotional growth and to reach maturity unscathed. It may be that in other sociological and cultural circumstances—in the simple and safe environment of a primitive South Sea tribe, for instance,—children are still able to enjoy an optimal childhood relatively unsupervised. Similarly, in our own society in the past—as during World War II, when great numbers of mothers temporarily left their homes to join the work force—society presented unsupervised children with fewer hazardous choices. But in the more complex, more adult-oriented society that exists today, unsupervised children must grow up faster and leave childhood behind simply in order to survive.

This is not to say that mothers who work care less for their children than stay-at-home moms. Many working mothers make a heroic effort to compensate for their reduced availability to their children, often by curtailing all adult-centered social opportunities that come up during nonworking hours in favor of family-centered occupations and pastimes. And yet many mothers and fathers who come home from a full day on the job are hard put to it to throw themselves into jolly family fun with the children; they simply don't have the energy. "I try to reserve quality time for my own children when I get home from work," says the headmistress of a New York private school who has herself commented that "people have less time for children these days—they're too busy fulfilling themselves." Continuing to speak about her own family life, she admits, "I'm often just exhausted when I get home. And many times I have to bring work home with me. There's just no way to avoid it. And so my most careful plans to devote myself entirely to my kids go down the drain."

One point must be emphasized: the observation that children have suffered a reduction of care as a result of women's increased employment is not meant to imply that women are to blame for choosing work over child care. Children *are*, indeed, required to grow up faster, to become more independent and self-sufficient, and face more danger if both parents work during the day; there is no reason to believe, however, that if the child's lot is easier with a stay-at-home parent, that parent *must be the mother.* Historically, mothers have been responsible for much of child care and child protection; as women today have sought to equalize their position with men, an unassailable goal, children have lost some of their traditional care. But the blame, if any is to be assigned, must go to men for not stepping into the breach and taking on a greater share of child-care burdens than they assumed in previous times. The fact is that men have not done so, in any significant numbers. Women cannot go backward and lose whatever equality they have gained. But in the interim, children must endure a different, less protected sort of childhood.

EIGHT

THE END OF MARRIAGE

The disappearance of marriage as a dependable, permanent structure within which children can live out their childhood is surely the most consequential change that has occurred in the last two decades. Before 1950 divorce was a relatively uncommon occurrence in families with children. By 1982 one out of every two marriages ended in divorce.

In spite of many nostalgic ideas about enduring marriages of the past, it is undoubtedly true that many of these remained intact out of economic necessity. There was a time when women had few alternatives outside marriage to ensure a comfortable style of living for themselves and their children. After the 1960s, however, new opportunities for women began to open up. As Heather Ross and Isabel Sawhill point out in their study of families headed by women,[1] women's new economic options were an important contributing factor in the rising divorce rate. Suddenly those women who had formerly accepted marital unhappiness as their inevitable lot, who had resigned themselves to inequality in marriage as the price they had to pay for survival, found an escape hatch. With new choices, open to them, they began to demand greater equality within their marriage. The power struggles that ensued did not improve the odds for marital longevity.

Other factors as well served to weaken the marital bonds of American fathers and mothers. New ideas introduced by the women's liberation movement created tension as "for better for worse" began to appear manifestly unfair to great numbers of women: the "worse" seemed to weigh more heavily on their shoulders than on men's.

Changes wrought by the sexual revolution caused marriages to be built on the volatile foundations of erotic gratification rather than on the stable bases of common interests, of shared backgrounds and religious beliefs. The stresses of a recession-prone economy, the mass uneasiness caused by political disillusionment and the ever increasing nuclear threat: all played a part in weakening the institution of marriage.

But finally it was a simple snowball effect that quickened the pace of marital disintegration. As divorce became more common, it simply became more acceptable to end a marriage by divorce. By the beginning of the 1970s divorce had become epidemic. In *The Last Picture Show,* a movie describing social aspects of small-town American life in the 1950s, the wife is asked why she remains married to a husband she detests. She answers, "I wasn't brought up to leave my husband. Maybe I'm just scared to." But by the 1970s, divorce was no longer something that "just isn't done." Now everybody seemed to be doing it, and splitting up became an accepted social phenomenon, like getting married or moving to the suburbs.

The number of children affected by divorce grows by the day. In the single decade between 1970 and 1980 the number of households headed by only one parent doubled, a change that officials of the Census Bureau attribute primarily to divorce. There were 956,000 families headed by divorced women in 1970; by 1981 this number had grown to 2.7 million.[2] Indeed, there is hardly a child today who is not painfully aware of divorce and its consequences, if not because his own parents are no longer together, at least through the unhappy experience of any number of his friends and acquaintances.

Must a divorce always be traumatic for children? The answer is probably yes. Under the best of circumstances a family breakup cannot fail to confound the very definition of childhood and to transport the child outside childhood's boundaries, while in a paradoxical way the parents assume the child's former place, at least temporarily. For nothing causes men and women to regress to a childlike state of helplessness and dependence more than the upheaval and turmoil that surrounds the end of a marriage. Each of the partners temporarily re-enacts basic childhood dramas and relives those primitive fears of rejection and desertion, separation and loss, that are experienced in the early years of life. Meanwhile the children of a troubled marriage bear a dual burden: not only must they cope with their own painful feelings of loss and resentment, but they must at the same time deal with the helplessness and misery that their parents cannot successfully hide from them.

In such situations the roles are often strangely reversed: the parents temporarily become children, and the child, in his raw encounters with adult unhappiness and his recognition of adult failure, is forced to become more adult. Even when the crisis is over, when reason once again prevails, when misery subsides, when the child may be ensconced in a seemingly happier family life within a new marriage, innocence will never be recaptured. The child knows what he knows forever.

TELLING THE " REAL TRUTH "

In the aftermath of divorce, some of the secrecy parents once instinctively maintained out of protectiveness towards children no longer seems advisable. Whereas parents used to feel that children did not need to be burdened with adult problems and unhappiness (the idea being that childhood should be a relatively carefree time), when divorce looms new strategies are advocated and adopted, ones that might have seemed destructive in an intact family situation.

"Give them the real truth," the experts advise. "Just telling the child that 'We don't love each other any more' is a copout," writes a child psychiatrist, who goes on to suggest, "Tell them the real reasons for the divorce, like 'Your father drinks too much,' or 'I've met someone else I care about more.' "[3] Another frequently offered piece of advice is "The parents should not hide their own distress." It seems important to the counselors involved with the children of divorce that the kids come to understand as completely as possible all the factors behind the divorce and all the possibilities that now exist for their future family life.

There are, indeed, compelling reasons for ending secrecy in a home where the parents are splitting up, the most important of which is to prevent children from believing that *they* are responsible for the divorce, that their naughtiness or stubbornness or whatever actually caused their parents to break up. This is a common reaction among children, a result of their normal egocentrism. Therefore, the experts propose, providing children with *the real truth* about the causes of the divorce will keep them from bearing an unnecessary and undeserved burden of guilt for their parents' marital failure.

To prevent such misunderstandings, children today, even very young ones, are let in on the secrets of their parents' deficiencies, vulnerabilities, failings, weaknesses, long before these might become naturally apparent in the environment of an unbroken family. Early disabused of their normal illusions of parental omnipotence and omniscience, children of divorce are made to understand in specific detail that their parents are often as helpless and confused as they themselves are. In the past, this was a discovery that children made slowly and painfully during the course of their adolescence; when they finally came to grips with the realization that their parents were just normal, fallible human beings, they were often ready to take the last step towards separating emotionally from their parents and starting an independent life. They were on the verge of adulthood.

But for children who have their parents' fallibility thrust upon them, as it were, long before they reach the developmental point of separation and independence, the question that becomes a deep part of the child's life, whether consciously articulated or not, is: Who will take care of me if my parents can't even take care of themselves? In this way the relaxed insouciance of childhood, during which the child can throw all its energies into work or play, is transformed into a more cautious, survival-oriented frame of mind, one, indeed, that is not unlike that which adults must always maintain—except, of course, for those rare times of relaxation, times when they can let go, times when they like to think they "feel like children again."

SHOOT THE MOON

A dramatic illustration of the adult world impinging heavily on children caught in the crisis of divorce may be seen in a recent movie,

Shoot the Moon, the first of a wave of divorce films to focus closely on the plight of the children involved.

As the movie opens the parents, though obviously troubled, still attempt to hide their marital problems from their four children. The husband, in fact, maintains a protective attitude towards his wife as well by hiding his extramarital affair from her. Though the film is set in "laid-back" California, nevertheless the children are seen to be leading a relatively structured life in which their roles as children are clearly defined; they go to bed at a regular time, for instance. In the first scene the parents make a great effort to maintain a solid front before the children, waiting to exchange their first angry words until they have left the house for the evening. Three of the children are blissfully unaware of anything amiss—they are playful and merry, going about their lives with that complete self-absorption only untroubled children can afford. The oldest child has accidentally learned her father's secret; in contrast to her younger sisters, she is a serious and brooding presence.

After the breakup, all the children rapidly lose their innocence. Suddenly nobody tries to hide anything from them. The parents air their grievances in front of the kids. When the youngsters spend weekends with their father and his girlfriend, the adults are in no way furtive about their sexual relationship; they openly kiss and hold hands in front of the children and make no bones about the fact that they share the same bed at night. Indeed, the girlfriend hurries the protesting kids to bed before their usual bedtime, cheerfully admitting that she wants them tucked away so that she can make love to their father. When they ask her what "sleeping with him" is like, she answers, to their disgust, "It's delicious, like eating ice cream." In time, the children's mother finds a boyfriend and does not hide the sexual side of that relationship from the kids either.

This open conduct of postmarital sexual life has become so common in contemporary America that it is easy to lose sight of the fact that parents of the past usually behaved very differently. Even ten or fifteen years ago divorcing parents continued to hide their new sexual involvements from the children as a matter of course, just as they had been secretive about their sex lives with their legitimate mates before the marriage dissolved. After a divorce they may have kept up a pretense that the new love object, if they had one, was a "friend," and as children became familiar with these "friends" of their divorced mothers or fathers, they were likely to call them Uncle Bill or Aunt Helen. It would have been unlikely for Mom to hold hands with Uncle Bill or kiss him in front of the children, much less talk about how "delicious" her sex life with him was! Eventually Mom or Dad might remarry, and only then did Uncle Bill or Aunt Helen take on a new definition as he or she moved into the conjugal bedroom.

This system, needless to say, considerably diminished the sexual opportunities of the partners in a broken marriage, especially of the custodial parent (almost invariably the mother). Conscientious parents, nevertheless, usually made the sacrifice; they believed it was their responsibility as parents to protect their children from knowledge of their sexual lives so long as these were conducted outside marriage.

Today, however, parents' love involvements following a breakup are often pursued openly in front of the children. The child in *Shoot the Moon* knows everything there is to know when she shouts angrily at her mother, "Last week you fucked Dad and this week you're fucking Frank. Who are you going to fuck next week?"

THE MOTHER'S SEX LIFE

Since most children remain with their mothers after a divorce, the mother's attitude towards her own sexuality becomes a matter of no small importance in the children's new home life. Women of the pre–sexual revolution era, whose life pattern before marriage had often been one of sexual repression, were far more likely to sacrifice their own sex life after a divorce, or at least allow it to be greatly inconvenienced, in order to "do right" by the children. But today's woman, who considers it her right to have a fulfilled sex life just as men have always done, no longer feels constrained to pursue that now questionable goal of preserving herself as a virgin, so to speak, in her children's eyes. The pure image once so much a part of the conventional model of a wife and mother seems rather sexist and dishonest today. Women now feel justified in being more open about their sexuality. And so it happens that in the new pattern that contemporary children live with of single parenthood, followed by courtship, remarriage, re–split-up, new courtship, re-remarriage, they are inevitably exposed to experiences, revelations, emotional ups and downs, and all the irrational aspects of human sexual relations that were long considered too hot for children to handle.

A New York mother raising two pre-teenage daughters after her divorce provides an example of children's new entry into the formerly secret world of adult sexuality: "As a little girl I had very little idea of what went on in the adult world. My parents were very hush-hush about sex, and so were everybody else's parents. We actually wondered whether they ever 'did it'! Now my kids know huge amounts about every aspect of my life—physical, emotional, even sexual. How can I keep it from them? I'm not going to give up a sex life because of them—I think that would be bad for all of us. But the first time a man spent the night after the divorce I was nervous about the kids' reaction. I got up early so I could be out in the other room with the bedroom door closed when the girls got up. When my eight-year-old came into the kitchen I was making pancakes, chattering about this and that. She looked at me and said, 'Mom, did you know there's a man in your bed?' She turned on her heels and took off."

Another recently divorced mother of two children, one who has retained certain protective notions of the past, describes her accommodation to her new situation as a sexually active woman: "I have some rules that I really stick to. Like if I've just met somebody and wanted to go to bed with him I would do that. But if the kids were home, either I'd bring him in in the middle of the night or I'd go somewhere else with him. I'd let the kids know I was sleeping with a man only if it became a serious relationship."

As a result of children's new knowledge of their parent's formerly secret sexual and emotional involvements, children of divorce acquire certain defenses that make them seem more adult than children appeared to be in the past. Trustfulness often disappears from their repertory of feelings.

Much of latter-day children's wariness is directed at the mother's new boyfriend. A man who found himself in such a position reports:

"When I first got involved with Fran, her kids, who were eight and ten, gave me a terrible time. They literally gave me the cold shoulder. Fran had been living with some other guy for the past three years and I guess they had gotten used to him, so they were downright hostile to me when I appeared. Meanwhile they're very verbal, very sophisticated kids. They certainly know a lot more about life than I knew when I was their age."

As it happens, this father has two children of his own from a former marriage who are about the same age as Fran's children. As he tells about his own children it becomes clear that it is not only the mother's sexual relationships that bring adult reality into the lives of children of divorce; though kids may live with their mother and be more privy to her secrets, they are rarely spared a deep look into their father's often disorganized and unpredictable sex life.

"My own kids are just as hostile when they meet a new girlfriend of mine," he continues. "They've been through a whole series of my crazy relationships after the divorce, and they know that I've slept with five different women. Now they're both very cautious. They don't know how long each relationship will last, and whether the new woman will really like them. They don't want to put their feelings into it. I feel terribly uneasy to think of the mistrust these kids have formed. They seem more reticent, more withdrawn than kids I see in regular families."

A NEW ROLE FOR CHILDREN

Not only in their interactions with their parents' new companions and their insights into the frailty of adult affairs of the heart do children today find themselves pushed out of childhood and into a precociously adult awareness of life. Another impetus comes from the altered relationship between parent and child in a single-parent household, where frequently the child takes on some of the functions that the absent adult in the house would have served.

"I know that I 'debrief' with the kids when I come home from work, much the way I used to do with my husband when I was married," says a divorced New York mother. "I suppose I need some sort of outlet, and the kids always seem so interested. So why not talk about things with them?" She partially answers her own question when she adds, "I guess I tell them more than I ought about my problems. They've begun to worry about our family finances. And whenever I tell them about troubles in the office I can see that they're panicked that I might get fired. But they might as well find out sooner than later that life can be complicated and unfair and infuriating."

Another mother, recently separated, relates: "I always feel a little insecure about how I look when I go out in the evening. I used to ask my husband about whether this dress looks all right, or whether my hairdo doesn't look odd. Now that we've split, I ask the kids how I look, just as if they were adults. And they're only seven and nine!"

The use of children as a sounding board may introduce subjects more upsetting than sartorial insecurity. "I had a series of terrible dreams the other night about my ex-husband having a wild sexual affair with some other woman," this same mother continues. "At breakfast the next morning I found myself telling the kids about the dream. I guess I just had to tell somebody. I could see that they were upset by it, by the whole notion of my anger at what their father might be doing, to say nothing about the very existence of our separate sex lives."

Sometimes it is the children themselves in the single-parent family who seek out a new role. A divorced mother of two school-age daughters in New York reports: "What happens is that I let things go a bit and all of a sudden I realize that the kids are encroaching on my sphere, that they're trying to be, either collectively or singly, the other parent. They want the input in the family that a father would have. They want a say in making the budget, in running the household. When I was a child we weren't even allowed to know how much our father made!"

On some occasions, children not only take on the role of the missing adult in the family but find that the customary roles are entirely reversed: they become parents, in a sense, to their own parent, who in turn becomes the child. A Denver mother recalls: "When I broke up with a guy I'd been going with for three years, my kids were really wonderful. I was a wreck, and my nine-year-old son would pat me on the back and say, 'It's going to be all right,

Mom,' while my eleven-year-old daughter took over the cooking and even brought me breakfast in bed! It was great for me. I don't know if it was so great for them."

A thirteen-year-old eighth-grader from upstate New York whose parents recently divorced offers a look at the realities of role reversal from the child's viewpoint: "It's sort of weird, but my mother is like my age sometimes. She's discovering things about life at the same time I am, having boyfriends, and having men sleep over. She even asks *me* questions about sex. This is very confusing for her, and makes me very confused too a lot of the time. And sometimes she's very strict, but then she's also very loose about things."

Some child experts take an optimistic view of children's new roles in today's changing families. Psychiatrist Paulina Kernberg feels that the potential of children to help parents has been underrated. "Children can participate in family matters to a far greater extent than people believed in the past," Dr. Kernberg asserts. "To share problems with children does not necessarily mean to unload. I feel that children can understand that parents have problems of their own, even serious ones such as mental illness. If the child is told things in language he can understand, by an empathetic adult, he can share many problems that were once hidden from children. A child needs to know he can do something, at least listen to a parent's problems, rather than be left to his own wild imagination. People forget that children are resilient and that they're potentially good pals."[4]

Other members of the psychiatric profession are not as sanguine about children's new roles. Psychoanalyst Katharine Rees considers the reversal of roles in which children give parents support and counsel to be ill-advised. "Even though children may be very astute and wise about their parents and their problems, their own lives are likely to be messed up when they get too involved in these adult affairs," Dr. Rees states. "Children are too needy and dependent themselves. A patient of mine, as a result of her parents breaking up, began to take on an inappropriately adult and advisory role towards both her parents and their sex life. Eventually she felt propelled into getting involved herself in a sexual relationship with a boy her own age, fourteen years old. She thought she was emotionally ready— after all, she was practically a parent of her own parents. But it turned out disastrously. At that point her parents should have been the important people for her, her main love objects. She should have been able to turn to them for the love and affection she so desperately needed. But the roles had become too confused in that family, causing her to go to someone her own age for fulfillment. Unfortunately the boy couldn't fill her emotional needs—he was too young as well."[5]

A divorced mother raising two pre-teenage children brought up another disturbing question in regard to the adult roles her children were assuming in her new-style family. "The kids give me a lot of support. I talk to them about all sorts of things that I wouldn't have dreamed of talking to kids about before I divorced. I really deal with them like adults a lot of the time. The trouble is," she added thoughtfully, "that the kids get confused when I try to deal with them like children again, when I tell them how to behave or when to go to bed. I'm not sure I can have it both ways, having them be so adult and then trying to act like a parent to them. What I'm really afraid of is not being able to control them when they get older and start getting involved with other kids and drinking and drugs and all that. I don't know what I'll do then."

THE   WAGES   OF   DIVORCE

As the population of children affected by family breakup and parental loss continues to grow, researchers as well as informal investigators are discovering that in many ways a family breakup increases a child's vulnerability to the stresses of modern life. Statistically, children of divorce are more likely to become involved with alcohol and drugs, to commit suicide, to get in trouble with the law, to fail in school. And as time goes on, new and troubling connections are being uncovered between the children of divorce and a host of grave social problems, from runaways to sexual abuse and even mass hysteria.

The director of a sanctuary program for runaways in Huntington, Long Island, finds that a large percentage of the children who seek refuge are from single-parent families, usually headed by the mother. Quite a few, she observes, are from "blended families" established by a second marriage. Hardly the jolly Brady Bunch kind of family portrayed on television, in real life these families of step-parents, half-brothers, and half-sisters are often, in her words, "hotbeds of jealousy, visitation problems, and financial worries."[6]

A troubling statistic appeared in a recent study of child sexual abuse conducted among 521 Boston families. Though children from every social class and ethnic and racial background seemed equally vulnerable to abuse, there was a significantly higher incidence of it among those whose parents had divorced and remarried.[7]

A recent investigation of a mysterious childhood "ailment" reported in a psychiatric journal[8] provides another indication that children of divorce are more vulnerable in many ways than children without an experience of loss. The heretofore unexplained condition under study is one in which large numbers of children at a school or camp suddenly become ill with symptoms suggesting exposure to a toxic or infectious agent; in all such episodes, however, despite extensive tests and examination, no cause for the outbreak is ever found. Within recent years this "disease" has been diagnosed as a kind of mass hysteria precipitated among children by an incident causing psychological or physical stress. The researchers studying a specific outbreak of such hysteria that occurred in a Boston suburb three years ago found that of the 224 boys and girls involved, those most severely affected were more likely to have experienced parental divorce or a death within the family at some time in their past. The psychiatrists concluded that childhood loss, whether by divorce or death, renders children more vulnerable to a stressful situation, causing them to react more violently. The children from intact families also succumbed to the contagion, but less severely; most of them did not require hospitalization. Although they may often give such an impression, the children of divorce, it appears, are not tougher than their more protected peers. They are more at risk.

NOT DIVORCED...YET

It would be misleading to assume that only the children whose parents actually separate or divorce are seriously affected by today's

rising divorce rate. When interviewed, many children of stable families reveal considerable anxiety about the possibility that their parents
might divorce someday. "I worry about divorce constantly ever since
I saw *Kramer vs. Kramer,*" a ten-year-old New York girl admitted.
"My parents had a fight the other day, and my mother walked out
of the house. I thought to myself 'This is it!' and I cried and cried.
But she had just gone next-door to the neighbors'." A fifth-grader
revealed a common feeling of insecurity when she said, "We're one
of those families that aren't divorced," adding, after a pause, "at least,
not yet."

The burden of divorce is often shared by children of intact families
when their close friends have family troubles. A mother describes
such a situation: "My daughter Elizabeth was greatly distressed when
her friend Nancy's parents split up. Nancy's reaction to the divorce
was to become enormously dependent on Elizabeth. She wanted her
to be with her all the time, became jealous of all her other friendships,
and Elizabeth didn't know how to deal with it. She's only ten, after
all. She couldn't take the emotional burden. She would come home
and burst into tears: 'I don't like Nancy, she's no fun any more, she
keeps writing me notes telling me that I like my other friends better.
She doesn't want me to talk to anybody else but her.' "

The cloud of anxiety about divorce that hangs over the heads of
all children today is darkened by the suddenness and unexpectedness
with which divorce often seems to strike. A twelve-year-old boy
reports a conversation with his best friend whose parents had suddenly separated: "I said to Danny, 'Didn't you know they were going
to break up? I'd know if anything were wrong with *my* parents.' And
he said, 'That's what *I* always thought. But you never can be sure.'
That kind of scared me, I guess."

"We have to reassure the kids frequently about our marriage," a
mother who has been married for fifteen years reports. "On the other
hand, when our thirteen-year-old was mad at us for not letting her
go to a party last year she said, 'Why can't you be divorced like
everybody else?' "

STAYING TOGETHER FOR THE
CHILDREN'S SAKE

Hardly anyone these days proposes that parents ought to stay together for the children's sake. While the conventional wisdom of the past had it that parents owed it to their children to maintain their marriage even if they were totally miserable with each other, a decided shift in thinking about the impact of divorce set in just as the divorce rate began its upward climb at the beginning of the 1970s. Nobody denied that it is hard on kids or that it causes anguish and leaves psychological scars. But gradually people stopped believing that divorce is the worst alternative and that if children are to grow up well they must grow up in an intact family. The new credo goes like this: An unhappy marriage is bound to bring equal unhappiness to the children trapped within it. If the parents are miserable, this will make the children equally miserable. Therefore it is better for parents to divorce and strike out for more personal happiness than to perpetuate an unhappy marriage "for the children's sake."

Today's child experts have consistently supported the new attitude. Peter Neubauer, an eminent child specialist and psychoanalyst, points out: "In the past, when divorce was not acceptable for social or religious reasons, the internal conflict was often incredible, though the intact family was maintained. The continuation of an unhappy marriage may have just as detrimental an effect on the children in the family as a divorce, maybe more so."[9]

Obviously, nobody denies that it is best of all for children to grow up with a mother and father happily married to each other. "We know that a warm, loving, intact family is the best thing for a child —you don't need a professional to tell you that," Dr. Neubauer continues. "But did such a thing exist on a greater scale in the past? I don't think so."

Parents of the past, however, stayed together. Even when they were desperately unhappy, they put up with their discontents in order to preserve a stable home for the children. Today's parents, operating according to different beliefs, have grown less and less willing to sacrifice their dreams of perfection and happiness for the sake of their children or to bear with each other's idiosyncrasies, differences, demands, foibles, or weaknesses in order to preserve the marriage. What is more, in an era of unprecedented concentration on self-fulfillment, each partner's heightened expectations for personal, sexual, emotional, and intellectual gratification within the marriage have not increased the chances that the union will prosper. Quite the contrary: such goals are likely to lead to disappointment and marital failure. How fortunate it is, then, that the experts no longer insist that children must have a stable family in order to grow up well. How convenient that they have reversed their position and now believe that the very remedy adults resort to when they are unhappy—divorce—will equally benefit the children.

The belief that divorce is preferable to an unhappy marriage for the children in the family reflects today's newly undifferentiated concept of childhood. The old attitude that prescribed staying together for the sake of the children was based on the supposition that children are a species apart, so different from adults that certain actions that might lead to adult unhappiness (staying together, though miserable) could nevertheless work to children's advantage. But under today's prevailing view that sees children as operating under the same rules as adults, an action that benefits the adults in a family (getting divorced) is therefore seen as beneficial for the children too. Conversely, if the parents are unhappy in their marriage and yet stay together, today's belief has it that this will be worse for the kids than if they split up.

Nevertheless, while few today deny that an unhappy couple may better their own lot by ending their marriage, there is room for doubt that the same holds true for their children. A recent longitudinal study of divorced parents and their children conducted by the California Children of Divorce Project strengthens this doubt. The researchers found that of the sixty divorced families involved in their project, most of the adults, after five years of separation, were still glad they had divorced. The majority of the partners, and especially the women, felt better off for having ended the marriage in spite of various economic hardships the divorce had caused. "Their self-esteem was higher and their overall psychological adjustment was considerably improved . . . many of their somatic symptoms and their psychological dysfunctions disappeared during the postdivorce years."[10]

The children, however, presented a different picture indeed, one that does not support Dr. Neubauer's optimistic view, one that dashes to the ground the illusions of today's divorcing parents who hope against hope that their actions are not merely self-serving but will prove to be good for the kids as well. In the California study the authors found, to their admitted surprise, that "many marriages that had been unhappy for the adults had been reasonably comfortable, even gratifying, for the children." They observed that "few of the children concurred with their parents' decision or experienced relief at the time of the separation." Five years later, while four-fifths of the parents were glad they had divorced, "over one-half of the children involved in the divorces did not regard the divorced family as an improvement over their pre-divorce family."

Furthermore, the authors write unequivocally: "Unlike the adults, who felt considerably improved after the divorce, the children and adolescents did not, as a group, show an improvement in their psychological health during the years following the separation." So much for the notion that the continuance of an unhappy family may be *more* detrimental to a child's mental health than a good clean divorce.

Finally, although the authors found that one-third of the youngsters were "lively, well-adjusted, and contented with the general tenor of their lives" five years after their parents' divorce, they found an equal number who were "unhappy, still angry at one or both parents, still yearning for the presence in the family of the departed parent, still lonely, needy, and feeling deprived and rejected." Moreover, although a number of the children under study were found to cope well and behave normally in spite of their parents' divorce, the authors nevertheless believed that *all* the children "had the sense of having sustained a difficult and unhappy time in their lives which had cast a shadow over their childhood or their adolescence . . . for all a significant part of their childhood had become a sad and frightening time."

As more and more parents divorce in their search for a more fulfilling and gratifying marital relationship, and as more and more of them *do* improve their situation—perhaps because of greater maturity and more realistic expectations the second time around—greater and greater numbers of children are suffering the consequences: a diminished childhood. "I felt like I was being thrown out into the world before I was ready!" cried a thirteen-year-old about her divorcing parents. And indeed, as the California study articulates about virtually all the children involved, "these youngsters felt that the time available to them for growing up had been dramatically foreshortened. They felt hurried and pressed to achieve quickly the independence which is usually achieved over several years. They felt deprived of playtime and a sense of leisure."

THE THERAPEUTIC MILIEU

Childhood was once seen as a time when the family provided safety and security and protection for the child, if for no other reason than that he was a child. Adulthood, on the other hand, was a time when one was out in the world and had to seek security for oneself. In the old-style family, the child ventured out of the family for experience, but as soon as he ran into trouble of one sort or another, back into the family he'd retreat to find comfort and warmth, to lick his wounds, to consolidate his losses, to simply be a child. But what happens, in an era of family instability and mounting divorce, when the family itself is the source of the child's problem? Now the outside world must somehow provide a therapeutic milieu for the child.

The trend today is away from trust in the innate benevolence of the family. As Dr. Michael I. Cohen, head of adolescent medicine at Albert Einstein Medical College, puts it, "with the family in disarray, we the professionals have finally come to grips with such situations as sex education and have told parents, 'If you're not going to teach your children about these things then we, as a society, will teach them. We'll offer them that information.' "[11]

School is frequently the first place where children's difficulties in dealing with their parents' divorce are observed, the parents often being too incapacitated themselves, or too busy, to take much notice. As one school counselor remarked, "At a time when the family is falling apart and it seems everything at home is changing, school often is the only stable and constant aspect of their lives." And a headline in a teachers' journal, "The Prevalence of Divorce Brings New Responsibilities to Teachers,"[12] indicates the growing awareness in the outside world of the change that has overtaken the structure of childhood for great numbers of American children, and the efforts schools are beginning to make to help children deal with their new problems.

But it is not exclusively for the child's benefit that teachers and other extrafamilial adults take an interest in helping children of divorce. It becomes ever more obvious that children from troubled families bring their deep problems into the classroom and create difficulties for the teacher and the other pupils. An upstate New York teacher reports: "There's been a tremendous increase in broken homes in our school. Over sixty percent of our kids are now from single-parent homes. You often see the situation where the mother has custody of the kids, and she's working at two jobs just to make ends meet, and maybe even going to school at night to better herself so she can eventually make it with one job. And so the kids are left to fend for themselves. They seem to develop a lot of anger, and we have to deal with it in the classroom. We see a lot of the 'If nobody cares about me then I don't care about anything' sort of attitude among these kids in our classrooms."

A sixth-grade teacher observes: "You can walk into my classroom and easily pick out the kids from stable homes. Those are the kids who come in ready for school, ready to respond, ready to really work at things. The ones who are lacking this sort of support at home, especially those whose parents have just broken up and are busy with their own messy lives, are often very hyper. They seem to need an awful lot of attention. They want to talk to somebody, anybody, just to talk! This certainly makes things harder for the teacher, because these kids want to monopolize our time and it's not really fair to the other kids."

In addition to teachers' consistent testimony about the problems brought into the classroom by children from troubled families, researchers have begun to focus more attention on the consequences of divorce. An ambitious study of over 18,000 students found that children in one-parent families showed lower achievement and substantially more school problems than children from families in which both mother and father lived in the home; these problems included infractions of discipline in the classroom, absenteeism, truancy, suspensions, dropouts, and expulsions. A subsequent follow-up confirmed the findings of the first study. Moreover, it made a new association between divorce and school troubles, finding that children in one-parent families were more likely to defy their teachers' authority than those in one-parent homes.[13] Yet another study, by the Center of Advanced Study in Behavioral Sciences, investigated the cognitive effects of divorce and found that achievement-test scores and school grades of children being reared in single-family homes tend to be lower than those of children living with two parents.[14]

Out of necessity, as the impact of divorce on school behavior becomes more evident, schools and other outside agencies are taking steps to ameliorate some of the effects of family breakups. From the first-grade show-and-tell sessions that deal these days with weekend daddies, parental fights, and mothers' live-in boyfriends, to school-organized group-therapy sessions for single-parent children dealing with the loneliness, anxiety, and feelings of abandonment that divorce often brings in its wake, schools are getting involved in areas that have never before been considered a part of their bailiwick.

A typical program designed to help children of divorce is a project at the Salem Elementary School in New York. As reported in the *New York Times* on February 19, 1980, this school makes available a special counselor to meet with children whose parents are separated or divorced, to allow them to "share their experiences and talk with one another about the problems particular to children in their situation." This is only one of hundreds of similar programs cropping up in schools throughout the country.

The purpose of these programs, as stated by one counselor, is "to make the children realize that the divorce is not their fault, that both parents still love them, that neither parent is the villain, that their feelings of divided loyalty and anger are normal, and that other children of divorced parents experience the same problems." As a result, great numbers of children for the first time are dealing with their psychological problems outside the family. An agency other than the family is intervening, is interpreting the parents' behavior to the children, is acting *in loco parentis.* Of course, school has long served as a substitute for parents during part of the day, ever since education became compulsory. But even those schools of the past that operated under the most progressive, psychologically oriented principles still incorporated these principles into their academic programs. Now schools, apart from their usual curricula, are addressing themselves to those psychological needs of children that more and more parents today seem no longer willing or able to satisfy.

As a result of such extrafamilial therapeutic opportunities, children *are* gaining valuable insights: that they are not alone with their problems, that their feelings are normal, that they did not cause their family breakup and need not harbor guilt feelings. As they gain information about their own feelings, they acquire such concepts as "emotional needs" and "displaced anger" and "divided loyalties." They study strategies for coping with angry or grief-stricken parents and learn how to avoid getting caught in the middle of a parental war. Consequently, many of them come to appear more "sophisticated," more "adult" somehow, than the others in their classes.

In fact, the increasing numbers of special arrangements offered to troubled children these days are in themselves a symbol of a grave loss these children have sustained—of childhood itself. For just as adults cannot hope to have their problems taken care of by their mothers and fathers, so too these children of broken homes are forced to look outside their families for help. No longer is their family a refuge, a bastion, a dependable source of solutions to all problems. In this way the childhood of today's children of divorce or separation has drifted closer to adulthood in its definition than childhood has been for several centuries.

THE
PURPOSE
OF
CHILDHOOD

*T*HE END OF REPRESSION

SEXUAL JACOBINS

O nce upon a time children seemed to be sexually quiescent during the years before adolescence. Even after everyone on all levels of society had come to understand Freud's revelations about sex as an underlying force in early childhood, still a distinction was inevitably made: there is sex and there is *sex*. No matter what Freud said, the Oedipus complex didn't seem like *real* sex.

Of course, there was always the same old evidence of childhood sexuality: Johnny was just as likely to play with his "little widdler" in 1940 or 1950 as little Hans in Freud's casebook had been a half a century earlier. But while by 1950 enlightened parents no longer threatened to cut it off when the child was found masturbating, still child experts and advisers and consequently parents continued to maintain a cautiously repressive attitude towards the free expression of childhood sexuality.

Examples of such an attitude may be seen in most of the popular child-care books of the fifties and early sixties. In Haim Ginott's best-selling *Between Parent and Child,* published in the sixties, we read: "Parents may exert a mild pressure against self-indulgence, not because it is pathological, but because it is not progressive; it does not result in social relationships or personal growth. . . . The child's main satisfactions should come from personal relationships and achievements."[1]

The very use of the term "self-indulgence" for masturbation reveals a continuity of attitude between Dr. Ginott and child experts a century earlier when a strong antisexual bias prevailed, an era when "self-indulgence" and "self-abuse" were common euphemisms for masturbation. Though Dr. Spock and Dr. Ginott and any number of other popular child-care writers spoke out bravely and openly about sex, about sex education, about sexual curiosity, masturbation, and the like, still they represented an enlightened continuation of the ideas of past generations, with the gentle suppression of childhood sexuality still the underlying principle.

And then, it seems, long after everyone thought that a very "modern" attitude about sex already existed, things really did change and an old way of thinking finally came to an end. By the 1970s sex had became a regular part of children's lives, partly through the uncontrollable medium of television, but also through books, magazines, and family newspapers, and most important of all, as separation or divorce began to reveal parents as sexually active people to ever greater numbers of children.

Children, not surprisingly, began to look and act less childishly. In a sexually inflamed society these former innocents commenced to gain a knowledge of sexual complexities most *adults* had not possessed a generation earlier. In some cases children embarked on a stunningly precocious sex life of their own, provoking much anxiety and a certain amount of niggling envy among their parents and guardians. Whether children, after this moment of change, simply ceased to hide strong sexual impulses that had always been part of their natural endowment but had previously been culturally suppressed, or whether they now were being stimulated into precocious sexual activity by the example of their equally overstimulated elders, is still to be determined. But by the 1970s it became impossible to ignore the evidence of a new sexuality among an age group that had, until recently, been considered so sexless and innocent as to be called "latent"—children known as preadolescents or schoolchildren or whatever.

As the events of the sixties cast their shadow upon so many parts of American life, those influential child experts whom American parents had long depended on for guidance began to reflect society's changed attitudes towards sex. As psychiatrist Thomas Szasz saw it, the era of the sexual Jesuits, the antisexual faction, was ended. The day of the sexual Jacobins, who promote the free expression of sexuality among young and old alike, had arrived.[2]

Compare the "Jesuitical" approach to childhood masturbation exemplified by the Victorian belief that the practice would cause insanity and hairy palms, or the Freudian tenet that it would interfere with the acquisition of knowledge, or the modern Ginottian warning that it could be a handicap to personal growth, with the new-era attitude that masturbation is a positive force in children's lives. "The natural way of testing the equipment, apart from being very enjoyable, and the way that nearly all boys and girls first learn what 'sex feels like,' write the authors of a recent sex-education book for parents and children, adding, "Unfortunately, and for reasons it is hard to understand, people have made an enormous fuss about this rather obvious way of practicing for adult sexuality." Another prosexual advocate, writing about masturbation, exhorts parents "not to look for it, nor to try to prevent it directly or even indirectly by attempting to divert the youngster's attention to other activities." (Diversion had been the common "Jesuitical" strategy of the enlightened fifties and sixties.) The most Jacobinic adviser writes: "Sex is pleasure. Pure, keen, clean, living pleasure. If a child is to be sexually healthy, parents must feel there is nothing wrong with sexual pleasure. Pleasure is 'wrong' only when it causes pain. Is there pain to anyone when a baby finds sexual pleasure at a mother's breast, or a child masturbates or enjoys genital play with another child, or a teenager taking good contraceptive precautions has warm, giving intercourse, who is being hurt?"[3]

In a virtual reversal of the old-style fear that free childhood sexuality would have damaging consequences, the Jacobins proclaim the dangers of sexual repression. While parents of the past went to great lengths to discourage their children from expressing sexual impulses, the parents of the prosexual era begin to feel equally uneasy if their children show no particular interest in sex. Something seems wrong if their child is *not* masturbating for some reason. "If we don't get rid of our Victorian ideas we may literally cripple our children sexually," is the current word from the experts. The leap from a belief in the crippling effect of masturbation to the crippling effect of nonmasturbation is a great one indeed.

CULTIVATING CHILDHOOD SEX

The prosexual advocates go further than trying to redress the wrongs of the past in regard to masturbation. A report from the Sex Information and Education Council of the United States (SIECUS) proposes that sexuality be *cultivated* during childhood, just as artistic or mathematical proclivities or sports interests ought to be cultivated: "Thus sexuality may become not only a fully accepted dimension of life but an emphasized one." The report goes on to suggest: "Sex is so good and important a part of life that if children don't happen to discover sexual enjoyment for themselves, if we really like them we will make sure they do."[4]

It is hard to gainsay the argument that if sex is a great and wonderful part of life, then children should not be denied its pleasures. And yet the true purpose of the new-era sexual message remains unclear. The specific sexual activities of preadolescent children mentioned in the SIECUS report are "masturbation, sex play with others of either sex or animals, nudity," and also the use of vulgar language. Is the idea, then, that children should be taught *how* to masturbate properly, or encouraged to masturbate if for some reason they show too little interest in it? Should conscientious parents not merely look the other way, as enlightened ones sometimes do, when their young children go off for a round or two of "Doctor," but rather hire a tutor?

The upshot of such advice has been the creation of confusion and guilt among parents torn by the opposing pulls of the old and the new attitudes towards sexuality. Their own parents were almost without exception more sexually repressive than they have learned to be with their own children. Thus they cannot simply follow their natural tendencies, based on their own upbringing—their attitude towards their own sexuality has changed, thanks to the far more liberal and open approach to sex that prevails today. Yet if they allow their child more sexual freedom than they enjoyed as children, indeed, if they go ahead and try to cultivate his or her sexuality as a talent to be developed, while at the same time (as is so often the case) they themselves do not feel as perfectly fulfilled sexually as they might wish, they may find themselves in the paradoxical position of feeling less adult than their own child. Sexual experience, after all, was always a great separator between adults and children. Parents' relationship with their ever more experienced and sexually liberated children may begin to take on the equality of a relationship with a peer. Or a new kind of inequality may develop as parents find themselves in a somewhat less than equal position vis-à-vis their worldly children ("Oh Mom, you don't even know what oral sex is!") It is not hard to understand why there is an almost palpable feeling of unease, sometimes tinged with hostility, about children's sexuality that is painfully evident among parents today.

THANK HEAVEN FOR LITTLE GIRLS

It has been observed that when people talk about "children growing up faster" and express anxiety about precocious sexual behavior, it is more often girls than boys that are on their minds. Lolita was a girl. The sexually provocative children displayed on TV commercials are little girls. The celebrated sex symbols—the Brooke Shieldses and Jody Fosters who as prepubescents were cast in sexual roles—all little girls. Meanwhile, in the national mythology prepubescent boys are generally perceived as carefree Huck Finns or eager Little Leaguers rather than as sexual prodigies. Generally it is girls who have changed their reading habits, preferring those "young adult" books by Judy Blume or Norma Klein about masturbation and "going all the way" to tales about horses and junior proms such as girls used to enjoy. Meanwhile, school-age boys stick to the sports stories and adventures they have always preferred. This disparity may exist because boys have always been raised somewhat less protectively than girls. Today, as parents turn from a protective philosophy of child rearing to a preparatory one, their behavior towards girls shows the greatest change.

Statistically, there is some confirmation for the observation that girls are changing more rapidly than boys on the scale of precocity. While there has been a steady decline in the age at which teenagers first have sexual intercourse, a number of studies indicate that this decline is accounted for mainly by earlier initiation of females. Boys, it seems, continue to follow much the same patterns as in the past; girls are simply catching up. Bruno Bettelheim was referring to the past's greater protectiveness towards girls when he declared: "Our modern educational and social system . . . forces girls into frequent and close association with boys on an equal footing, and without any of the traditional modes of protection. Although girls now live with just as much exposure to the world and are just as unprotected by family as boys have always been, we somehow expect, or at least wish, that this fact should have no impact on girls' sexual behavior. Such an expectation is clearly unreasonable."[5]

Nevertheless, many parents continue to feel protective towards girls even while they are unable to maintain a protective environment for them. A recent study by the Harvard Project on Human Social Learning shows that less than 30 percent of mothers want to convey to their daughters the idea that premarital sex is acceptable, while almost 60 percent want to communicate to their sons that it is all right.[6] Fathers show a similar double standard in their attitudes: less than 40 percent of fathers want their daughters to feel that premarital sex is acceptable, but 70 percent feel favorably disposed towards it among their sons.

It appears that not only were parents once more restrictive towards girls' sexuality than boys' (quite understandably in light of the unequal burden girls bear of the consequence of premarital sexual activity—pregnancy) but that in certain ways parents, and especially fathers, did not discourage—indeed, encouraged—a certain amount of sexual precocity among boys. The new visibility of homosexuality in American society during the last two decades has greatly exacerbated this tendency.

OUT OF THE CLOSET

For many years after modern parents agreed that it is better to teach "the facts of life" during early childhood, the particular fact of homosexuality continued to be kept from young children. Indeed, even in the adult world homosexuality was once so veiled in secrecy that before adolescence most children were completely unaware of its existence, though there might have been homosexuals in their close family circle.

Today this has changed. In an era when any number of sit-coms during the "family hour" on television feature "odd couples" and the issue of gay rights appears on the news with regularity, it would be hard to avoid homosexuality as a subject of discussion. Even pre-schoolers may be heard calling each other "faggot" in the schoolyard.

Children's new awareness of homosexuality has not failed to create a certain amount of anxiety among preadolescents. Not having achieved sexual maturity, and with no way of physically testing their sexuality as adolescents can do, they suddenly begin to worry and wonder whether they may turn out to be "faggots" themselves. This anxiety manifests itself in much teasing about homosexuality among today's schoolchildren.

A fifth-grade teacher observes: "Homosexuality is a big thing among fifth-graders—there's constant talk about it. The word 'gay' is used all the time. And the kids tease each other by imitating what they consider homosexual gestures—you know, the limp wrist, or licking the finger and stroking the eyebrow, that kind of thing."

"The kids in my class are confused and anxious about homosexuality," another fifth-grade teacher says. "When they get angry with each other they put each other down by saying, 'Oh, you pervert!' The other day I moved my hand in a certain way and two girls started giggling. When I asked them why, they said, 'Oh, Mrs. Gonzalez, you look gay when you do that!' "

Friendships between children of the same sex are not infrequently affected by the underlying anxiety about sex orientation that sets in several years before puberty these days. A sixth-grade boy describes a painful experience: "My friend Barry and I went through a very rough time earlier this year. We've been friends for years, but we're not really part of the regular group of kids. Suddenly all the kids started teasing us—'Oh, you two must be gay!' I came home crying a couple of times. It just made me so mad."

Indirectly, in its impact on parental attitudes towards children's sexuality, the new visibility of homosexuality in American society since the 1960s may be deeply implicated in some of the changes that have overtaken contemporary childhood. Certainly the pronounced shift in modern child rearing from an antisexual, repressive style to a prosexual style may be seen to be connected with parental attitudes towards homosexuality.

It would be a mistake to think that because there is greater acceptance of homosexuality and a genuine movement towards homosexual rights in American society today, parents have somehow changed their basic, underlying feelings about their children's sexual future. Most parents continue to have an abiding desire that their children grow up to be heterosexual, that they marry and have children, and thus provide them a pathway to immortality. This desire is probably part of an instinct programmed into the human race, with clear survival value for the species. During past eras, when homosexuality was not a public issue, parents simply assumed that children would grow up to be heterosexual. Fathers, to be sure, carried on a bit about the masculinity of their sons, encouraging them to behave "like a man," not to be "a sissy." Little girls, likewise, were supposed to be ladylike and maternal and to play with dolls rather than to climb trees. But these attitudes that promoted sex-stereotyped behavior among children were part of a general parental aim to promote certain accepted forms of behavior—to make their children grow up in their own image, as it were. In general parents followed the somewhat repressive patterns that had prevailed when they were children, without fear that this might in some way influence their children's future sexual orientation.

When homosexuality became an open subject, parents began to feel increasingly uneasy about their children's sexual development, and especially, their children's heterosexual orientation. The writings of the experts, moreover, made it clear that the ways parents handle children in their early years can have a great effect on their sexual future. For example, the authors of an influential textbook on sexuality, *The Cycles of Sex*,[7] write as follows about the latency period:

This is the period in which forerunners of future homosexual adaptations often first appear. In most instances these disturbances in sexual identity were initiated in earlier phases, as a result of family interactions which failed to foster a secure sexual identity that includes a firm expectation of heterosexual behavior. Now there may be evidence of a child's avoiding the usual and expected activities appropriate to his sex.

"Failed to foster a secure sexual identity" . . . dread words to a parent's ear! In contrast to the past assumption that children *naturally* develop into "normal" adults, today's parents have suddenly had to face the unpleasant possibility that they may have done something wrong, that they may *still* be doing something wrong, and that now their child will never provide them with grandchildren. To make the matter worse, newspapers and magazines, television and the movies, remind parents of these anxieties at every turn by focusing more, year after year, on the subject of homosexuality. It is easy to understand why parents of the 1970s and 1980s shifted from a repressive child-rearing style that tried to delay the emergence of sexuality to a style that in a number of ways worked to develop sexual precocity: they needed to have their fears about their children's sexual future allayed as soon as possible. Even among parents of pre-school children anxiety about sexual roles and orientation is not uncommon. The father of a five-year-old reports: "Most of the parents who are willing to talk about it will admit that they are worried that their son will turn out to be 'one of them.' They joke about it at various parent meetings at our nursery school. Another father said to me the other day, 'Thank heaven Jimmy has a crush on Susie. It looks like he's going to be all right.' And that's really the way most of us look at it."

Reflecting these fears, experts today are encouraging parents to allow the sort of sexual acting-out that was once strictly forbidden. The authors of *Cycles of Sex* warn:

> One subtle anti-heterosexual message may be communicated by a parent's anxiety over opportunities for heterosexual play. It is almost unheard of for children to be permitted to spend the night with friends of the opposite sex. Adults are suspicious of any privacy between a boy and a girl. It is rare that parents fail to show serious disapproval when pairs or groups involving the opposite sex are found examining each other's genitals. Yet frequently having friends of the same sex spend the night together, with uninterrupted opportunities for sex play, is approved and unquestioned by most parents, and part of the normal experience of most schoolchildren. The implication that heterosexual activity is more taboo than homoerotic play is clear and often impresses itself upon the children.

Driven by anxiety about their role in their children's sexual development, many parents today do not dare to *show* disapproval of heterosexual sex play of the kind described above even when they continue to *feel* disapproving. And in direct as well as subtle ways, parents have begun to encourage heterosexual activities among children in early puberty or considerably before. A New York mother, whose first marriage had ended in divorce after her husband revealed a homosexual preference, encouraged the son of her second marriage to form special friendships with girls from his early elementary school years, and did not hide her delight when he began to "date" and have "real girlfriends" when he was in sixth grade. She talked to an interviewer about her son's sex life with unmistakable pride: "Chuck lost his virginity this year. I know a lot of people think thirteen is too young, but I think it's fine, so long as the kids know what they're doing and don't get pregnant. Of course I told Chuck about birth control. But I also gave him a few tips about how to please a woman sexually. I think he'll be a great lover!"

A mother who learned that her fourteen-year-old son was having a sexual relationship with a fifteen-year-old girl reacted with ambivalence—first shock and then clear relief: "Though it kind of knocked my socks off when I found out, a part of me was glad that it happened, I have to admit. His uncle, his father's brother, is homosexual, so one part of me felt that this [the sexual experience] was a step in the right direction."

A mother of three apologized for her middle child: "Michael isn't into girls yet. You see he's really very involved with school sports." She felt a need to justify her son's lack of interest in girls. The boy, as it happened, was nine years old.

Children themselves speak, often with not a little disbelief, of their parents' anxious encouragement of heterosexuality. A sixth-grader reported: "My parents are always saying: Do you have a girlfriend yet? Do you have a girlfriend yet? They're always asking."

A fifth-grade classmate told a similar tale: "I told my father I was going to a movie with my brother, and my father asked me, 'Don't you want to take some girl?' He seemed disappointed that I didn't want to."

THE PARENTAL DILEMMA

Parental ambivalence about their children's sexuality is clearly seen in Kathryn Watterson Burkhart's recent book *Growing Into Love*, [8] an illuminating look at contemporary teenagers and their thoughts and behavior. On the one hand the author encourages that side of the ambivalent parent that wants everything to be pretty much the same as when he was a child. To this yearning ear she writes:

> There's no doubt that many of our young adolescents *hear* about somebody in their class or in the class ahead of them who is sleeping around, who is into drugs or sex in a serious way. They know about homosexual activity and oral sex and other things that would have shocked our grandmothers, but they're basically just kids groping for their identity. They may have seen many pictures of nudes, they may have seen people in bed together in the movies, but that doesn't mean they will personalize the infor-

mation at this point in their lives. Having information doesn't mean acting on it.

The parents no doubt breathe a sign of relief. Nothing much has changed, it appears. On the other hand, the book abounds in statements from children and teenagers that could not conceivably have been uttered openly (or even secretly) a generation ago:

When I got my first boyfriend, I was fourteen. He was the first boy I had sex with. It was pretty good, but he noticed that if we'd been smoking and then got into sex, I'd get all stiff and it was terrible. He got very confrontive about it, so after a while, I would never smoke pot when we were going to get into sex.

Confused and ambivalent parents may well wonder whether they are doing enough to foster their children's optimal sexual development when they read vignettes about free and sexually fulfilled teenage couples such as Tom and Betty ("I felt like my body was going to go crazy, it was so exciting") or Clair and Tommy ("I knew his body quite well by then and he knew my body quite well, but this was the first time he'd seen my body in full sunlight") or Brenda and Jack ("When he got back we went into my room and got into bed together, and were nude, and he did it to me"), and quite a few others. And in case parents wonder whether all this delicious teenage sex might create problems in later life, Burkhart is reassuring:

Certainly it seemed to me that many of the teenagers I talked to would have fuller and richer marital lives because of the healthy patterns they established in premarital experiences. Many said that even without intercourse, what they had learned about their sexual responsiveness and about foreplay would eventually contribute to a more complete experience. Others, who had begun to have premarital intercourse, also seemed to have learned and grown through the experience.

Thus we may trace the etiology of the current tension between parents' hopes that kids really *are* the same as ever, that most of those distressing reports filtering out of the media about the numbers of twelve-year-old girls and boys "doing it" are mere myths, and their contradictory hopes that indeed their children *are* doing it, doing it beautifully in full sunshine, and doing it better than their parents ever managed to.

The parental dilemma is not made easier by the common assumption in many advice books today that sex is one of those skills, like piano playing, in which one never develops a real proficiency unless one begins to take lessons early. Moreover, parents are informed by the experts of some of the consequences their children might suffer as a result of excessive sexual repression, among them school phobia, sleep disturbances, exaggerated religiosity, obsessive-compulsive behavior, and finally, complete genital anaesthesia.

Some experts go so far as to suggest that in today's increasingly indifferent society, sexual gratification may offer children some compensation for their deprivations. Prepubescent sex may even become "an alternative to the generally pointless regimentation, humiliation and boredom of school," one author notes. And yet . . . though most modern adults will hasten to agree that sex is a wonderful thing, they still cannot help but hestiate about joining the sexual Jacobins. Some deep-rooted instinct holds them back, prompts them to keep their children sexually latent as long as possible, and makes them feel deeply anxious when they find that they cannot.

RETARDING SEXUALITY

There was a time when adult society was close-mouthed about sexual matters, when best-selling novels contained no explicit descriptions of strange sexual acts, when children's books dealt with bunnies and treasure hunts, not incest and gang rape, when all movies were eligible for a G rating, when sexual fulfillment was not the *ne plus ultra* of American couples—fifteen or twenty years ago, in other words. In those days it was far easier to maintain children in a state of sexual latency during their childhood years. And indeed, until recent years a widespread desire to retard children's sexual development subtended many everyday child-rearing practices.

The notion of trying to repress children's sexuality and delay their entry into adulthood has a long history. Among the earliest exponents of this idea was Jean-Jacques Rousseau, who influenced child-rearing and educational directions in the late eighteenth century perhaps as much as Freud has influenced those of our time. Rousseau proposed a slow, steady, and protected regimen in childhood expressly in order to avoid stimulating a child's sexual curiosity. By this means, Rousseau believed, the onset of puberty would somehow be delayed. This attitude, leading directly to the fear of precocity so characteristic of the nineteenth and early twentieth centuries, may still be found lurking behind parental anxieties today, especially those having to do with sexual stimulation via material on television or in books and magazines.

Many of the puzzling child-rearing practices of the past begin to make sense when we understand that their hidden purpose was to delay the child's sexual development. Take, for instance, that peculiar and yet not uncommon pattern among middle- and upper-class parents of the past century of maintaining their children in a permanent state of undernourishment, if not actual semistarvation, during much of their childhood. An eloquent recollection of such a childhood that took place, as it happens, in a Scottish castle as recently as the 1930s describes a situation of hunger in the midst of plenty that was the common lot of great numbers of privileged children of the past:

> Mealtimes held another ever-present fear—that of not getting enough to eat. At the Home Farm—the one that existed for the sole purpose of providing the castle with produce—the fat cows lowed in their stalls, letting down steady streams of rich, creamy milk, while in the five-acre kitchen garden, three gardeners labored over regimented lines of peas and beans, lettuces and cucumbers and asparagus, cabbages and spinach. Raspberries and strawberries and plums and damsons and cherries and grapes poured into the house every summer morning, carried shoulder-high by barefoot garden boys, while in the winter the gamekeepers, their leather trousers stained by the blood of their victims, impaled on the sharp hooks in the game larder the twitching legs of deer and hare and the curled, twine-tied claws of pheasant, partridge, snipe, duck and grouse. Towards the sea rolled the fields of ripe oats, soon to be ground between the flat stones of the village mill; potatoes and turnips and carrots lay heaped in earth-covered mounds, while pigs and calves and lambs died, protesting noisily, in the pens behind the cow shed. All this activity was for the purpose of feeding the people in the castle, yet we children were almost always hungry.[1]

While most people assume that the practice of underfeeding children was based on some sort of Spartan principles intended to toughen children, it may actually have been motivated by a very different purpose indeed. As we may see in the following passage written in the 1830s by Sylvester Graham, an influential advice writer for parents, a curious connection was once made between food deprivation and sexual retardation:

The delicate susceptibilities of youth being constantly tortured, and their young blood continually heated by a *stimulating* and *depraving* diet, their sensual propensities are more rapidly developed than are their rational and moral powers. . . . Among the causes of extensive and excessive self-pollution [a Victorian euphemism for masturbation] . . . the most important are, 1. Improper diet —the free use of flesh (meat) with more or less stimulating seasonings and condiments . . . all of which unduly stimulate and irritate the nervous system, heat the blood, and early develop a preternatural sensibility and prurience of the genital organs, and 2. Excesses in *quantity* of aliment. Were our children kept in the plainest and simplest manner, unless they were restrained as to quantity by their parents or guardians, they would be exceedingly *apt to eat more* than they *really need* . . . this not only promotes permanent injury in the digestive organs, but the whole constitution is much impaired by it, *and the sexual appetite rapidly developed and strengthened.* Overfeeding is a powerful cause of early concupiscence and licentiousness as well as of innumerable other evils. [Italics added][2]

Few today would subscribe to the notion that certain foods stimulate sexuality in children. And the idea that the *quantity* of food consumed by a child might "strengthen the sexual appetite" sounds positively bizarre to our ears. Nevertheless, there *is* an established connection between nutrition and a child's sexual development. During the last century a considerable amount of evidence has accumulated indicating that in Western Europe and in the United States there has been a significant acceleration of sexual development. Research shows that the average age of menarche (the onset of menstruation) was around sixteen a hundred years ago; today it is twelve-and-a-half.[3] The most widely accepted explanation for this acceleration is nutritional. Researchers propose that there is a specific connection between a girl's body weight, specifically the proportion of fat tissue to muscle, and the onset of puberty. In the two or three years before menarche, fat tissue increases 125 percent. The critical weight for menarche seems to be somewhere between 98 and 103 pounds. When the critical weight, or the critical proportion of fat to muscle, is reached, this seems to trigger the hormonal mechanism that activates the pubertal process. There is an important adaptive advantage to this weight requirement: both pregnancy and lactation require large reserves of body fat if the health of mother or baby is not to be jeopardized.[4]

At first glance the nutritional explanation for so great a change as a four-year decrease in the age of menarche in a single century doesn't quite make sense. Granted that the nutritional standards for poor children improved over a hundred years, what with better social welfare systems, higher standards of living, free school lunches, and the like. But what about the offspring of the comfortable and rich a hundred years ago? We have only to look at cookbooks and dinner menus of that era to see that the middle and upper classes enjoyed a rich and varied diet, one likely to lead to the acquisition of that critical weight all too soon. Why, then, didn't those children reach puberty at approximately the same age as their counterparts today? The answer may lie, at least in part, in the abovementioned under-feeding of children practiced by precisely those upper-echelon parents who read the advice writers such as Sylvester Graham. And while there wasn't a jot of scientific truth in the pronouncements of those Victorian gurus that rich foods or ample portions would pro-duce "a prurience of the genital organs," nevertheless the purpose of avoiding precocious sexuality was achieved: children were fed a scanty diet and the onset of puberty (certainly for girls and probably for boys as well) was delayed by a number of years.

STRENUOUS EXERCISE

Delaying puberty by means of semistarvation is not a policy likely to attract a large following today. But a recent recommendation for solving the troubling problem of teenage pregnancy shows that the idea of delaying the onset of puberty still has its advocates. According to Rose Frisch, a researcher at Harvard and an expert on the physiol-ogy of puberty, current research demonstrates that regular, strenuous physical activity significantly delays menarche in girls. What better way to forestall the baneful possibility of early teenage pregnancy than to simply delay fertility for a few years? How much easier than trying to instill the values of chastity in hot-blooded youth, for instance, or to train children to use birth control via early sex education. For this reason Frisch suggests that schools adopt a program of rigorous athletic training for children beginning in the early elementary grades.[5]

Strenuous exercise, it is likely, works to delay menarche in the same way that semistarvation worked: by postponing the achievement of that critical fat-lean proportion necessary to trigger the onset of puberty. Yet an hour of gymnastics a day is clearly more healthful than a hunger regime. It is a fact that child prodigies in the athletic sphere—young skaters or gymnasts—generally reach puberty considerably later than the average nonathletic child. Perhaps this simple solution, if widely adopted, might succeed in ameliorating the difficult social situation brought on by the ever increasing numbers of teenage pregnancies. By postponing some of the parent-child problems that arise at adolescence, delayed puberty might have other far-reaching benefits for society. It might, by prolonging the physical duration of childhood, allow children to acquire experience, to gain emotional maturity, before being confronted with the confusions and conflicts (some of them hormonally induced) that puberty inevitably brings.

FEAR OF PREGNANCY

It is not as if child sexuality has always been universally feared in the human community. We know that in other historical times and other cultures children's nascent sexual impulses have been casually accepted as part of the human baggage along with all their other developing capacities. In the Middle Ages, for instance, adults for their own amusement often encouraged children's sexual explorations. Anthropological evidence reveals cultures in which children's normal sexual behavior is completely acceptable, where masturbation, group sex play, and imitative copulation among children are considered perfectly normal. Why, then, has there been such a long history of antisexuality in what might be called modern times, and why, as child sexuality has begun to emerge from its cloak of latency, do so many adults continue to feel anxious and uneasy about it?

Perhaps the most compelling force behind an antisexual bias is the fear of the consequences of precocious sexuality: early pregnancy. In the community-organized society of medieval times, as well as in the simpler social structures of primitive societies, an early-teenage pregnancy would not have been much more disadvantageous than a later-life pregnancy. In the complex social structure of postindustrial society, however, the negative consequences of teenage childbearing are many. From every point of view the current outlook is poor for the future of young love and its products: the mortality rate is higher for infants of teenage mothers—and the younger the mother, the higher the infant mortality rate. The health of the mother herself is endangered by early childbearing. Early parenthood greatly decreases the young parent's chances of attaining a higher level of education, and thus jeopardizes her occupational future. If a teenage mother and father decide to marry, their marriage has a poorer chance to survive than the marriages of older partners. Finally, the offspring of young teenagers are at a considerable disadvantage all by themselves: statistically their cognitive development is slower, and they tend to have more social and behavioral problems than children with older parents—even parents a few years older.[6]

Good reason to try to delay children's entry into sexual activity, and perhaps the one underlying a good deal of parental anxiety about childhood sexuality.

EMOTIONAL UNREADINESS

When one tries to understand the antisexual bias that informed so much of the child-rearing methodology of the past, even to the point of half-starving children or half-scaring them out of their wits with tales of the dread consequences of masturbation, it is important to consider the possible disparity between precocious physical and sexual development and the child's emotional and cognitive maturity. For as sexual maturation sets in earlier and earlier, parents fear that this physical precocity is not accompanied by a similar intellectual or emotional acceleration.

A mother comparing her own childhood development with that of her nine-year-old daughter articulates some of the problems of a unilaterally accelerated sexual development: "Tina is well developed. She has little breasts and pubic hair, and the doctor says she'll probably get her period early, maybe within a year. Well, she'll be ten, and I was thirteen when I got my period. But I was already at a very different point intellectually when I was thirteen. I was reading romantic books about womanhood, thinking about human relations, wondering about life. Tina is still at the animal-loving stage, reading *Black Beauty.* She thinks: Menstruation, yuch! To me it seemed like the threshold of romance. I keep wondering whether those additional years of intellectual growth might not make a thirteen-year-old more capable of dealing with all the confusions and frustrations of adolescence than a nine-year-old or ten-year-old."

Another mother observes: "I recognize so much about Helen's behavior—her frustration and anger and extreme sensitivity. Whenever I say something, she flings herself out of the room in tears. But I was fourteen when I went through that, and she is ten-and-a-half! It's as if she's missed three years of childhood!"

A more practical consideration feeds the anxieties of a New York father who worries about his eleven-year-old daughter's precocious signs of sexual development: "My concern is that Lucy may get ahead of herself. She may have all the trappings of maturity—make-up and eye-shadow and heels—and then be forced into a dangerous situation because she *looks* like she can handle it. Boys might ask her out for dates, for instance, before she's ready. Or she might be given too much responsibility in school because she *looks* more mature than she really is."

Quite simply the problem is this: though children reach puberty earlier, their cognitive and emotional development has not necessarily accelerated at the same pace. In Piaget's terminology, the child at the age of eleven or twelve may still be at the egocentric stage, rather than at the more reality-oriented stage that sets in around thirteen or fourteen. Thence may spring the common parental fears that the child is not ready to deal with sexuality, that he or she is emotionally unprepared, and other such concerns that seem to plague the parents of children on the verge of puberty today.

It is not only for the *child's* protection, however, that so many parents feel an urge to repress childhood sexuality, but for their own purposes as well. Since childhood is that period, in modern society, when the child must be transformed from a creature completely governed by instinct to a being who is able to control his instincts at will, whose very existence may depend on such control, and since sexuality is the area in which adults themselves continue to face problems in instinct control, parents hope that if the issue of sexuality is put off as long as possible, at least until puberty arrives and maybe considerably later, they will have a better chance of socializing their children and educating them, of imparting good values and ideals to them—in short, of maintaining their authority as parents.

INCEST

It is not only anxiety about whether the child is prepared to deal with the complexities of sexuality that causes parents to try to delay the child's sexual awakening. It may be that the parents' own sexual impulses are involved in their instinctive desire to prolong childhood and hold back the child's entry into full sexuality.

For if, as Freudian theory has it, children underneath their downy-faced, innocent exteriors are seething bundles of incestuous desires towards their mothers and murderous impulses towards their fathers (boy children, that is; girls supposedly feel just the other way), then clearly it becomes a sensible, even life-saving policy to keep those desires as latent and covert as possible. We might thus explain why some societies have shown an instinctive fear (even before Freud pointed out the Oedipus complex) of allowing sexuality to surface during childhood.

But in reality the prepubertal child is manifestly incapable of real sexual action (apart from innocent playing with the little widdler, etc.) and is, with very rare exceptions, unlikely to engage in any murderous doings. One great purpose of suppressing child sexuality, then, is to avoid the possibility of stimulating the *parent* to sexual exploitation.

Once an unthinkable subject, incest, as it happens, is much on people's minds today. Where once sexual relations between parents and their own children was the subject of tragedy, as in Sophocles' *Oedipus Rex,* today tales of cheerful and unpunished incest appear in a number of art movies *(Le Souffle au Coeur)* and, more recently, in the best-selling P. D. James novel *Innocent Blood,* in which an incident of incest, rather casually mentioned in the last chapter, proves to have a therapeutic effect on the young heroine. Besides the increasing appearance of salutary incest in literature and art, the subject of actual sexual attraction between parents and children has left the confines of pornography to become an acceptable area of concern for child-care experts and parent advisers. "It's perfectly normal to have sexual feelings towards your own child," is the reassuring word for parents, with just the smallest caveat added: "But mind you don't carry it too far."

Nonetheless, apart from the lunatic fringe (like the René Guyon Society in California, which promotes, in a truly crackpot manner, all sorts of child-adult sex and proclaims as its motto: Sex by eight or it's too late), and in spite of expert opinion as to the normalcy of the sexual attraction between parents and children, actual incest is still considered a form of child abuse, an act with devastating impact on a child's development, the ultimate exploitative act in which a dependent and immature child is involved in sexual activities it cannot fully comprehend.

It is surely not coincidental that there is so much attention being paid to incest at a time when cultural influences encourage child sexuality and children's behavior has become, if only by imitation, more sexually provocative than in the past. It may be seen that some of the strongest cultural and societal checks on incestuous relations have been notably diminished in recent years and the subject of incest has become one of real and active, rather than latent, concern in great numbers of families.

For a most extreme example of how cultural factors may serve to hold in check the sexual attraction between parents and children, consider the practice of baby swaddling that was universal several

---

*A film historian has counted *six* movies on the subject of incest in the 1920s, 1930s, and 1940s and *seventy-nine* in the 1960s.[7]

centuries ago, the binding of infants from head to toe with soft but firm bands of material, thus keeping them covered and immobilized for much of their early lives. If we are to go along with those child experts today who believe that babies sometimes provoke an erotic response from adults who handle them, this will certainly be less likely to occur when the child is a little bundle of starchy linen than when it is a warm, naked bit of squirming flesh.

From what we know of parent-child relations during the Middle Ages, a period when children lived in dangerous proximity and intimacy with their parents, commonly sharing the same bedroom and perhaps the same bed, the lack of psychological closeness that inevitably developed in a society in which children were separated from parents at the age of seven or eight, and in which children were incorporated casually into the adult world at about the same age, made incest less likely to occur than it might have under such circumstances within a closely bound family.

A very different check on incestuous family relations developed during the era that followed, the period when childhood emerged as a special time of life and when family relations became far more intimate than in preceding times. During this long period of growing psychological closeness between parents and children, a new factor helped parents keep their sexual distance: the maintenance of ignorance as an almost sacred part of childhood, the strict exclusion of children from all sexual matters and experiences, the protection of children from the acquisition of any sexual information, and the resulting preservation of children in a state of seeming sexual neutrality for as long as possible—as long, indeed, as they were to remain in the close family circle. During that era a child remained somewhat childlike almost until she or he left the nest for the wide world. Again, a parent is less likely to feel that "natural" attraction towards a child who has been taught to repress all sexual feelings, and who, in its dress, its speech, its manners, its entire demeanor, has been maintained in a state as far as possible from anything adult and sexual —a state of "childhood innocence."

Today, of course, children are not only less repressed than during Victorian times or than even twenty years ago (as adults are less repressed themselves ever since the sexual revolution), but thanks to their great exposure to television, they have picked up adult sexual mannerisms that they employ naturally in their walking and talking and general physical behavior. The restraining influence of innocence has been effectively removed. What is more, the restraining power of the taboo is failing as the thought of incest as something monstrous and abnormal is slowly replaced by the realization that such feelings are not uncommon. And though in recent decades the family as a solid and close entity has changed, has become more fragmented, nevertheless children's contact with their parents, though they may be divorced or remarried or never married, is psychologically intimate, far from the casual relations of the fifteenth and sixteenth centuries. Indeed, the very fragmenting of the family aggravates the problem, since parents in a broken family are far more needy of affection and comfort and nurture than parents in an intact family. And who happens to be around and available for succor to the frustrated parent? The unrepressed, sexually inviting son and especially daughter, that's who.

L ATENCY AND LEARNING

FREUD AS VICTORIAN

*I*t is not simply the fear of teenage pregnancy or fear of incest
or fear of emotional unreadiness that leads parents to look askance at
early sexuality and wish to delay the onset of puberty—to stall for
time, as it were, until their children have "more sense" than to get
into *that* sort of trouble. There is another feared consequence of
childhood sexuality that has bothered parents and educators of the
past and that continues to influence adults today through an unexpected mediator—Freud himself. The fear is not of what sexuality
might *cause*, such as pregnancy or venereal disease or the like, but
rather of what it might *prevent*. Specifically, there has long been a
notion that if a child is allowed to advance sexually, he will not make
good progress intellectually; he'll be a great lover at age twelve,
perhaps, but he'll never get into Harvard.

We are prepared to find this connection made by the nineteenth-
century advice writers. We are surprised indeed to find it intact in
the writings of Freud.

We tend to think that the concept of the child as an innocent,
sexless creature belongs to the long-ago Victorian era and that
Freud's ideas inaugurated an era in which childhood sexuality was
accepted as a reality, and as a good thing. Oddly enough, while
Freud's writings introduced the shocking new concept of infant
sexuality and investigated the sexual nature of *early* childhood, his
view of the years between toddlerhood and adolescence presents a
picture almost as innocent and idealized as any Victorian's. Freud
called these years the *latency period*. Only today, in a time when our

views have changed, can we see that the Freudian concept of a latency period represents a continuity of thinking about childhood that goes back for several centuries. As we observe the reality of today's children who are no longer sexually latent, it is clear that a new concept of childhood is at hand.

According to Freud's theoretical structure of personality development, there is a period of heightened sexuality during the first four or five years of life—the so-called Oedipal stage, when the child develops a sexual passion for the parent of the opposite sex. This, however, is followed by a stage in which that sexual energy diminishes, or at least goes into deep hiding, not to reappear until adolescence. This calm between two sexual storms covers the years between five or six and the onset of puberty at around twelve or thirteen, the very years that are commonly thought to make up the heart of childhood.

There was always a bit of a puzzle about this particular part of Freud's theory. Among all other creatures in the animal kingdom development generally proceeds in a steady line from immaturity to maturity. Why, then, in the human species alone should there be this sudden hiatus of five or six years between two spurts of sexual growth?

Freud developed an elegant answer for this self-created enigma, one that helped keep the idea of sexual latency flourishing long after other vestiges of Victorian thinking about childhood innocence had vanished. The latency period, he believed, has an evolutionary purpose: to serve the growth of civilization by allowing the child to devote his childhood to learning instead of to the development of his sexual capacities. The two, apparently, can not go on simultaneously. In other words, if the sex drive were allowed free expression during childhood, the child wouldn't be able to address himself to less exciting tasks such as memorizing the multiplication tables or learning the five principal products manufactured in Rochester, New York. In *Three Essays on Sexuality* Freud spelled out his belief that the two processes, intellectual development and sexual development, would interfere with each other: "Historians of civilization appear to be at one in assuming that powerful components are acquired for every kind of cultural achievement by this diversion of sexual instinctual forces from sexual aims and their direction to new ones—a process which deserves the name of 'sublimation.' "[1]

At this point we begin to revaluate our idea of Freud as an advocate of free sexuality during childhood, for in his latency theory he makes a connection between child sexuality and child educability that can't help but remind us that he was in many ways a product of the thinking of his times.

Consider the nineteenth-century belief, as found in the popular books for parents by Sylvester Graham, that when children are indulged in too rich a diet their "sensual propensities are more rapidly developed than are their rational and moral powers." The curious, and not inevitable, presumption underlying this notion is that the human organism cannot develop in two directions at once: if one drive is allowed free reign, the other must risk retardation or atrophy. This mechanistic, one-drive-at-a-time concept has influenced our thinking about child development in any number of ways, especially our attitudes towards child sexuality. It underlies most of the tension parents feel today about their children's sexual development and feeds their indecision as to whether they ought to repress sexuality or actively promote and encourage it.

It appears that the latency theory bears an odd kinship to Sylvester Graham's belief that only one drive can develop at any one period during the child's development. Just as Graham declared that the moral and rational powers of the child must ebb if the sensual propensities are allowed to rise, so Freud suggested that if childhood sexuality is allowed to emerge, the child's ability to learn and acquire culture must diminish.

SCYLLA AND CHARYBDIS

While Freud seemed to suggest at first that the latency period had been evolutionarily programmed into the human race as a physiological reality, many of his later writings imply an understanding that sexual latency is not necessarily a natural part of childhood development but rather the result of society's active repression of any manifestations of sexuality in children. This repression may be accomplished by means of child-rearing strategies, by the elimination of opportunities for sexual exploration, or by a careful control of the child's environment to avoid sexual stimulation of any sort.

We find it startling to imagine that Freud threw in his lot with the promotion of sexual repression during childhood. After all, we trace so many of our contemporary beliefs about the damaging effects of sexual repression to his writings. What about Little Hans, whose nurse threatened to cut off his "little widdler" if he persisted in playing with it and who developed the most terrible neuroses as a result? Surely if he had been allowed to grow up free and untrammeled he would have been better off. Doesn't the modern trend towards nonrepression in child rearing trace directly to Freud's ideas?

Part of the problem lies in Freud's own ambivalence about latency. His early thinking did indeed suggest that certain adult neuroses were caused by specific environmental causes—by actual parental repressions such as threatening to cut off the widdler or imposing harsh toilet training or allowing the child to witness the primal scene. Freud suggests that these neuroses might have been avoided if these behaviors had been eliminated. But then, it appears, he changed his mind. By the mid-1930s he had come to believe that little could be done to mitigate the force of the various infantile conflicts, that the neuroses brought about by the clash between the child's instinctual needs and his parents' repressive requirements were not the exception but the inevitable rule. By 1933, Freud was already taking a stern position in regard to child rearing: "The child must learn to control his instincts . . . education must inhibit, forbid and suppress."[2] This was a far cry from the advocacy of free sexual expression in childhood that so many parents and educators believed (and still believe) to be part of Freud's intellectual legacy. Even the idea that early enlightenment about "the facts of life" might mitigate adult fixations was rejected by Freud himself in mid-career when he ruefully noted that "the prophylactic effect of this liberal measure [early sex education] has been greatly overestimated . . . for a long time after [children] have been given sexual enlightenment, they behave like primitive races who have had Christianity thrust upon them and who continue to worship their old idols in secret."[3]

Anna Freud summed up Freud's final position by stating that without a latency period and without repression, "there is a danger that [the child's] development will be retarded or interrupted, that he will rest content with gratification instead of sublimating, with masturbation instead of learning, that he will confine his desire for knowledge to sexual matters instead of extending it to the whole wide world."[4]

We begin to see that our image of the father of psychoanalysis as an ardent advocate of diminished repression during childhood is a distorted one, that indeed his fear of allowing the sex drive to emerge unhampered during childhood was as strong as, if not stronger than, that of the society into which he was born. As he wrote in "The Question of Lay Analysis": "Among races at a low level of civilization, and among the lower strata of civilized races, the sexuality of children seems to be given free rein. This probably provides a powerful protection against the subsequent development of neuroses in the individual. But does it not at the same time involve an extraordinary loss of the aptitude for cultural achievements? There is a good deal to suggest that here we are faced by a new Scylla and Charybdis."[5]

There is little question but that Freud opted for the Scylla of repression over the Charybdis of cultural loss. For while the fearful anti-masturbationists of the nineteenth century predicted a population of hairy-palmed lunatics if childhood sexuality were not suppressed, Freud feared an end to civilization itself and a return to a savage state of nature if this force were given free rein during the course of childhood.

A STATE OF NATURE

"I reject Freud's notion that there is a relation between sexual latency and an ability to learn," says Dr. Anke Erhardt, a psychoendocrinologist at the New York Psychiatric Institute. "Latency has never existed. Children were always, to a certain degree, sexually active. There is certainly no basic shift of energy from intellectual aspects to sexual ones, when children are not repressed sexually. It's only a matter of distraction, if they are made to feel enormously guilty or ashamed of their sexual activity."[6]

While the mechanistic, one-drive-at-a-time explanation of why sexual latency might make the child more educable may be debated, there is nevertheless evidence that latency and learning *are* closely connected. Consider the outcome of the progressive schools that sprang up during the early days of the psychoanalytic movement in the 1920s and 1930s. These schools hoped to prevent the development of adult neuroses by abolishing repression and allowing the child to behave freely, according to the dictates of his own instinctual drives. (Although Freud himself, as we have seen, eventually rejected the idea that repression could be eliminated from the childhood experience, even his closest disciples seem to have chosen to ignore this change.) These schools tried to help the child deal with the Oedipal conflict, gave sexual information freely, placed no restrictions on masturbation or sex play, replaced all authoritarian rules with permissive methods emphasizing reasoning and explanation. The teachers were trained to offer love and affection lavishly—a far cry from the rigid pedagogical standards of the time. But the results were paradoxical and distressing. According to Willi Heffer, a founder of The Kinderheim Baumgarten, one of these psychologically enlightened institutions, the children soon showed themselves to be "less curious about the more complicated world of objects." As he described them further: "They had no perseverance, they seemed egocentric, group demands affected them little. They were extremely intolerant of the demands of adults; timetables, mealtimes, table manners, routine hygienic measures, even if leniently handled, became sources of conflict." None of the changes Freud assumed children would undergo when they left early childhood and settled into the latency stage seemed to materialize—no greater docility, no eagerness to learn. Indeed, Heffer observed that the children showed "an unexpected degree of irritability, a tendency to obsession, depression and anxiety."[7] These, as it happens, are all traits we associate more with adults than with children. Children are usually angry, not irritable; persistent rather than obsessive; unhappy rather than depressed.

It begins to seem that the natural unfolding of children's behavior, were they to grow up in a state of nature (for that is not far from what the children of the Kinderheim Baumgarten enjoyed), might be very different from the process that occurs within the protective confines of a structured family. There, as the child's behavior is molded and repressed in order to make it conform to adult needs, the child feels safe, and may devote his attention entirely to work or play. But alertness, caution, as in a jungle, must be the watchwords in the unstructured and unprotected world where children are given free instinctual and emotional rein. Anxiety, irritability, suspiciousness— how far these emotions sound from our conception of the natural feelings of childhood. Yet these are just as natural to children when they are unrepressed and free of those limitations that the adult world traditionally imposes on them, and has imposed for the last two centuries. In a state of nature, children cannot afford to be childlike, to relax, to romp and play, to explore, "to be curious about the more complicated world of objects," above all, to *learn*.

PRODIGIES

Although we may trace Freud's latency concept to its nineteenth-century antecedents, and although we may disavow a physiological basis for the need for sexual suppression during childhood, must we therefore discard the idea that latency and the child's ability to learn are somehow connected?

It may cast some light on the purpose of sexual latency to consider a category of children in whose lives the connection between latency and the acquisition of learning and skills is exaggerated and therefore more obvious: those aberrations of nature referred to as "child prodigies."

We frequently see an odd phenomenon among child prodigies: although the child's amazing area of preternatural skill is admired and encouraged, the parental impulse to push or exploit the talent is inevitably balanced by a relentless holding back of any development in the sexual sphere. While the young prodigy develops skills on the piano or violin or the parallel bars, much is also made of the fact that he or she is, still and all, a "real child." In dress and deportment and in emotional dependence on the parents or guardians the prodigy is unvariably kept even more childlike than other children of the same age. The parents will often emphasize, in the frequent publicity that surrounds such prodigies, how happily he or she plays with trucks or dolls when not performing before the cheering throngs at Carnegie Hall. It begins to appear that some sort of one-drive-at-a-time notion not unlike Freud's latency theory is operating here: the parents sense that only by keeping down the sexual energies, by delaying the onset of puberty, will the child's marvelous talents be allowed to flourish in all their fullness. And as it happens, they are right. The onset of puberty is, indeed, the end of the road for every child prodigy. It marks the beginning of a journey toward adult artistry that only the rare *Wunderkind* makes successfully. But not because the sex drive eliminates the creative talent. The reason is more complicated.

The amazing talent of a child prodigy emerges without any of the ratiocinations that adult artists must invest their craft with. The child performs naturally, instinctively, out of some wellspring that he has direct access to. With puberty arrives self-consciousness. The child can no longer perform without understanding *how* he does it. Now he must relearn, re-examine, and make greater efforts to reach those depths that he plunged into so easily in his unconscious childhood.

But the parents' instinct to delay puberty is not only based on fear of a future loss of ability. They understand clearly that only if the child is maintained in a state of emotional dependency within the family can they successfully continue to protect and guide and educate him—to say nothing of developing his talent, which, in the case of such a gifted child, usually means making him practice a great many hours. Any striving towards a more adult level of emotional or social functioning would necessarily interfere both with the child's unselfconscious artistic expressiveness and with his willingness to do the work required to bring his skill to its highest possible level.

Not all parents, of course, have the opportunity or even the desire to help their child develop an extraordinary talent. But most have an understandable desire for their children to succeed, to do well in school, to excel in some area, to develop some talent, though not necessarily a prodigious one. It may well be that the strong aversion many parents feel towards signs of social precocity and their discomfort at early manifestations of sexuality indicate an instinctive under-standing of a connection between latency and the development of skills that lead to later achievement and success. Their fear of precocity may also be based on their observation that those children whose life circumstances have forced them to abbreviate childhood and allowed them much freer access to sexuality than their more protected counterparts are often the most troubled. For while precocity in artistic or intellectual realms strikes many parents as desirable, the other sort of precocity observed today does not seem to have survival value nor to bode well for a successful future in our society, a future that depends on the acquisition of skills and learning during childhood.

DIVORCE AND LEARNING

Further confirmation of a link between latency and the child's ability to learn is often discovered during times of family crisis, especially when parents separate or divorce. At such times the parents' attention inevitably turns away from the children and towards their own im-perative emotional needs. Moreover, many parents try to make up to their children for the trauma of separation by suspending certain familiar rules and structures, allowing them to stay up later, for instance, or to watch formerly forbidden television programs or to eat previously restricted junk foods. Finally, owing to the economic stress of a divorce, many, indeed most, custodial parents must resort to work outside the home in order to make ends meet. The conse-quence, for great numbers of children today, is the onset of a "state of nature" not unlike that of the children in unrestricted, psy-choanalytically inspired schools such as the Kinderheim Baum-garten.

Once again, under such conditions the child's ability to learn is clearly affected. Teachers today rarely fail to bring up the negative impact of family disintegration on children's schoolwork. Again and again they confirm that trouble at home causes trouble in school. A teacher states with certainty: "I can *always* tell when something has gone wrong at home by the way a child works at school. For instance, one of my students, Sandy, seemed more introverted this week. Her mind wasn't on her work. She just didn't focus on anything. Then I learned that her parents had just split up." And the teacher of a special class for kids with learning disabilities tells: "At least 75 percent of the kids in my class are from troubled families. I don't think I have a single classic learning-disabled kid in my class, with brain dysfunction, etcetera. Most of my kids are having such terrible problems at home that they can't concentrate on schoolwork."

In a most practical sense, moreover, divorce has a negative impact on children's school careers. As we have seen in chapter 8, children of divorce tend to be absent and late to school more frequently than children of intact families. The connection is not hard to see: in a well-functioning family parents do not find it difficult to get the kids off to school on time. The fact that children in single-parent families are more likely to be late or to play hooky indicates the child's changed position in such a family, with less parental control, less insistence that the child conform to rules of behavior. The child is given more responsibility over his own actions, as if he were an adult; quite understandably, he is likely to dawdle, to procrastinate, and to be late for school more often than a child in a more regulated family. The effect on the child's education is sadly obvious.

PROLONGING CHILDHOOD

lthough experts today are beginning to cast doubt on the physiological reality of Freud's concept of a latency period, it is in many ways a moot point. If latency does not occur naturally during the course of childhood, the history of the last several centuries demonstrates that it can, nevertheless, be imposed culturally. This is accomplished by maintaining secrecy about sexual matters and through the kind of strict inhibiting, forbidding, and suppressing that Freud himself advocated. But regardless of whether it is physiologically or culturally induced, does a latency period serve a particular developmental purpose in a child's life? Does it directly promote learning in the way Freud suggests? Those who reject the latency concept find fault with the notion that sexual development and intellectual development cannot go on simultaneously. Why not? they ask, not unreasonably.

But perhaps a period of sexual latency during childhood serves an indirect function: perhaps something about the child's sexlessness and sexual innocence during latency influences *adult* behavior towards children. That is, if cultural influences encourage repression of children's sexuality, the child's consequent appearance and demeanor will elicit very different responses from the adults around him than if he were allowed to behave in a more open and sexually advanced way. Here some biological evidence may be introduced to lend strength to the idea that the way adults perceive children does profoundly affect the way they behave towards them.

As Konrad Lorenz[1] has observed, children possess certain physical characteristics, unique to them, that change as they grow older. Lorenz used the term "neotenic" to describe these characteristics peculiar to the youthful stages of humankind, a word that had originally been applied to a condition of prolonged immaturity or arrested development seen in certain animal species. Among these neotenic traits are the child's outsized head relative to the rest of its body, its outsized eyes relative to the size of its head (an adult's eyes take up less of the entire face than a child's), the short, rounded proportions of its arms and legs. Lorenz proposed an evolutionary purpose to account for the fact that children are not merely miniaturized versions of adults but possess these specific differences in shape and form: these very traits, he suggests, act as innate "releasing mechanisms," causing adults instinctively to nurture and protect the child.

Stephen Jay Gould[2] enlarged the concept of neoteny in an essay tracing the evolution of the cartoon character Mickey Mouse from its earliest appearance in the 1930s to its final versions in the 1950s. The physical image of Mickey, he observes, changed steadily in the direction of neoteny; that is, year after year the artists accentuated those features of the cartoon mouse that were most juvenile. Thus the 1950 Mickey had a larger head in proportion to his body, larger eyes in proportion to his face, chubbier arms and legs than the 1930 or 1940 mouse. And as a result, Gould concludes, the character became more lovable to the reader. While the 1930s Mickey seemed shifty, mean, and aggressive, the 1950s Mickey seems naïve, cuddly, and adorable. The ratty tweaker-of-pigs'-nipples Mickey, as he appeared in the early 1930s, has changed into an inoffensive, childlike character who cannot even subdue a squirting clam. Gould believes that the Disney artists unconsciously applied the biological principle of neoteny and by doing so caused Mickey Mouse to make his way into the hearts of millions of American viewers. The sight of those juvenile features causes "an automatic surge of disarming tenderness," serving to make the humanoid rodent one of the most popular cartoon figures in history.

In addition to these special *physical* neotenic characteristics, Lorenz describes specific *behavior* traits displayed by the young of a species that have a powerful, genetically programmed effect on the adults of that species. The wide-beaked clamor of baby birds in the nest, for instance, has been shown to trigger off especially attentive feeding behavior from the parent birds. Conversely, if the baby birds for some reason refrain from opening their beaks extra wide and desist from their plaintive peeping, the adult birds will not feed them with reliability. In an experiment in which the parent birds were blindfolded and thus unable to see the gaping mouths of their young, they completely neglected to feed them, and the fledglings perished. Even across species lines these special behavior traits of the young— the insistent peeping of birds, the gamboling of puppies, the desperate tagging along of calves and colts—arouse feelings of protectiveness, for not only does the sight of childlike behavior among children elicit warm feelings among adults, but even the sight of young animals at play seems to touch some wellspring of tender emotion.

Neither Lorenz nor Gould specifically examined the behavior of the young of the human species from the viewpoint of neoteny. Yet there are obvious neotenic behavior patterns among humans just as there are among birds or beasts, things that children do which differ significantly from things that adults normally do and which similarly elicit a tender, nurturing response. Among these might be classified the speech patterns and language distortions of young children during the early stages of language acquisition—the little lisps and "cute" mispronunciations, the comical reversals (such as "pasghetti" for "spaghetti") that adults have long smiled at and repeated to each other with amusement; the abandoned romping and playing children spontaneously engage in that adults often stop and watch with special pleasure. And just as young animals have programmed into their behavior patterns certain signs of dependence and submissiveness that they display to older and stronger animals in order to avoid being treated aggressively—laying the ears back, dropping the head, placing the tail between the legs—so children have long shown submissive and dependent behavior to adults: a certain reticence or timidity, certain formulas of "respect" such as the use of "sir" and "Ma'am," "please" and "thank you"—learned behaviors that also fall into the neotenic category. The child's apparent latency or asexuality and its innocence of adult sexuality, another behavior that makes it distinctly different from the sexually active and knowing adult, may be regarded as a neotenic trait as well.

All these "childish" ways have an importance in children's lives that goes beyond simple custom or tradition. By provoking specific reactions among the adults in charge of the child, neotenic behavior promotes a particular kind of protectiveness towards the child. This, in turn, allows the child to pursue its various profitable activities, its exploration, and play—indeed, its entire education—in safety.

THE WONDER OF CHILDHOOD

The idea that there are certain "childlike" behavior patterns that elicit protective and nurturing instincts in adults is supported by a recent study showing that the very decision to have children in the first place is affected by adults' perception of children as "childlike" creatures.

A researcher studying the reasons why women choose to have or not have children found that many of the women who admitted to anxiety about parenthood brought up the specter of "bored, sophisticated children who have all the answers." Conversely, the most enthusiastic would-be mothers spoke of their desire "to experience the honesty and freshness of a child" or "to participate in the miracle of childhood."[3]

If the child's very existence, in some cases, depends on the parents' expectation of specifically childlike behavior, imagine their disappointment when that "honesty and freshness of childhood," the very thought of which brought them so much pleasure and the reality of which elicited from them, as we have suggested, the most tender care, suddenly is transformed by some malign alchemy into the sophisticated, bored, know-it-all behavior so prevalent among children today. Perhaps parents might be spared some of that disappointment if they were able to understand that certain aspects of childhood's specialness, that honesty or freshness or joy, may be connected to a particular developmental period when children really *are* qualitatively different from adults, and that the only way to carry these qualities over into later stages of childhood may be by cultural means.

There is no doubt that during early childhood the child really is amazingly different from the adult in almost every way—physiologically, cognitively, emotionally, perceptually; indeed, it sometimes appears to be a different species of human being. Unless the child has been drugged into an unnatural state of consciousness by phenobarbitol or excessive television viewing, the world really is strange and mysterious and full of wonder for a three- or four- or five-year-old. Rarely does one hear of a bored and jaded preschooler. This is the age, as well, when the child's physiological realities differ significantly from adults'—when neotenic traits conspire to make young children, by their very appearance, touching to an adult's eye. That childish waddle, that large head, those big eyes, those adorably chubby limbs: all these make the adult observer melt with sentimental emotion and provoke in him a desire to take care of the child.

And then, by the age of six or seven, a drastic transformation in the child's thinking occurs. He comes to discover that he is not the center of the universe but that there is another world outside himself, that his parents are not appendages at all but separate persons, and that the outside world is not a magic one but one governed by certain discoverable laws. In other words, the child's thinking begins to resemble adult thinking, in its form if not yet in its complexity. In Freud's structure, at this point the child has resolved the stormy Oedipal conflict and has settled into a rational and reasonable period of sexual latency. In Piaget's model, the child graduates from the preoperational stage to the stage of concrete operations.

Physically, by school age, the child has taken on the proportions that will characterize the adult form. No more toddle: the child now picks up many of the physical mannerisms of the people around him. It's often comical to see a seven-year-old boy walking along beside his father. Without consciously imitating, the boy walks with just the same little swagger, or bounce, or slump; his arms swing in just the same way; he swipes at a fly with the same careless gesture. The child's language, too, has come to resemble an adult's. All the baby mannerisms, the lisps, the *w* for *r*, the *y* for *l*, have vanished. The peculiar syntax—Baby go store, and so on—has become indistinguishable from simple adult speaking patterns. And just as the parents' physical mannerisms are adopted by their children quite automatically, so their speech patterns, accents, and finally even specific turns of phrase and verbal affectations are taken on, and seem quite natural coming from a school-age child.

From this point on, the "wonder of childhood" is far more of a cultural artifact. This is not to suggest that seven- or eight-year-olds are just like adults, that they do not have developmental needs that differ from those of adults (who also, as it happens, have developmental needs!). There is still the disparity in size and the important difference in sexual characteristics and capabilities. There is also, in modern society, a great educational gap between most adults and schoolchildren. A multitude of obvious disparities in judgment, understanding, perception, and interpretative capacities exist as well. Nevertheless, from this time on the child's conformance with or divergence from adult patterns no longer depends on innate physiological abilities and inabilities. By seven or eight, the child's brain chemistry has achieved its final state and no longer differs fundamentally from an adult's. This may, in fact, be the underlying basis for the fact that up until this age the child is essentially different and that after this age it is, for all its immaturity, essentially the same as an adult.

Although it would be difficult, a seven-year-old *could* survive on its own, *could*, theoretically, find some sort of shelter, *could*, let's say by crafty stealing, manage to get enough food for life sustenance. Obviously, this is not the case for a three- or four-year-old.

If the child is reared in a certain way, the cultural gap between it and the adults in its society can be prolonged. Its experience can be carefully limited to exclude those adult understandings that seem most distant from the child's original, age-specific perceptions. The child's magical thinking, for instance, can be prolonged by an absence of information about life's realities and by means of stories of the stork that brings babies, the Sandman who puts children to sleep, or Santa Claus. In the past many children believed some versions of these tales almost until adolescence.

For well over a century, the differences between childhood and adulthood were sedulously maintained. Children were read tales of fairies and magic. Once they began reading for themselves, they were given stories of talking animals or improbable humans such as "our friend the policeman" (who bore very little resemblance to any real-life cop). Children's clothes, too, were different: short skirts and hair ribbons and special-style shoes for little girls, and short pants and then knickers and finally long trousers or overalls for little boys.

One of the most important differences, the sexual disparity, was emphasized above all. Children's separation from the world of adult sex was once fairly complete. All aspects of sexuality, even the most elementary, were carefully withheld from them. In the past, even a country child could reach the age of twelve, as B. F. Skinner recounts in his autobiography, and still be completely surprised at the sight of his first unclothed woman to observe that she didn't have a penis. (He assumed she had one tucked between her legs.)[4]

When great areas of mystery in the child's life were still preserved and when a great many of life's hardships, complexities, and ambiguities were carefully excluded, it is not hard to understand that the qualities which still keep their hold on the imagination of today's prospective parents—that childlikeness, that honesty and freshness and naïveté—were preserved and seemed to be the child's natural and inevitable heritage. It is not hard to understand, then, the shock that contemporary adults feel when their seven-year-olds wiggle their hips in imitation of disco dancing they see on TV, when they ask questions about cunnilingus, when they seem so sophisticated, so far removed from their parents' nostalgic and romantic image of childhood of the past.

REPRESSED CHILDREN

When we think about the influence of childhood repression on human development, a curious contradiction becomes apparent: often children brought up under the most repressive circumstances seem to react to the requirement for adultlike impulse control, not by behaving more like adults, but by being more childlike.

Consider the realities of growing up in the Victorian era. When we read the diaries and childhood memoirs of people who were raised in a state of sexual repression and ignorance based on moral standards that even today are defined by the word "Victorian," who as children were often subjected to cruel treatment by rigid relatives (see Kipling's story "Baa, Baa, Black Sheep" for an almost unbearable picture of such cruelty) or by sadistic nannies whose own sexual repressions found an outlet in tyrannical mistreatment of their charges, we are often amazed to find that these children nevertheless created for themselves, when left to their own devices, a childhood paradise of games and innocent pleasures that they looked back to, in adulthood, with considerable nostalgia. Excluded from the adult world by the hierarchical conventions of the times, Victorian children threw their energies into a world of the imagination, organizing doll parties and waging toy-soldier wars. They incorporated the flora and fauna of the natural world—dogs and cats and rabbits and ducks, and even flowers and trees—into their elaborate fantasy life. These occupations, so different in every way from those of adults, sharpened the difference between childhood and adulthood, giving the young a distinctly more childlike aspect than the more permissively raised children of the eras that followed.

In Laurence Wylie's highly regarded book *A Village in the Vaucluse,* [5] a study of life in a small rural French village in the 1920s, this seemingly paradoxical juxtaposition of severe repression and free and spontaneous behavior frequently crops up. In the village school Wylie describes, for instance, the village children are required to sit still at their desks for hours at a time. They are regularly compelled to copy pages and pages in neat handwriting into their notebooks, an occupation most unnatural to the instincts of children as we understand them today, requiring much repression of their need to move about, to experiment, to explore, to "learn by doing." When lunchtime comes, however, these repressed French schoolchildren romp and play and carry on in the most childlike and unselfconscious fashion, playing games and running races. In contrast, their contemporary American counterparts have spent their morning in the jolly atmosphere of their open classrooms where they rarely have to do anything they haven't been "motivated" into doing. Yet *these* children, when released from their apparent childhood paradise, manifestly behave more sedately. They seem more mature, more adult.

One might reasonably expect it to work the other way—that children allowed free release of their childish instincts, children unrepressed, unforced into any adult mold, would behave with joyous childish abandon, while children forced to behave in ways contrary to their nature would be preternaturally adult as a result. But precisely the opposite occurs: the free child loses some of its childishness, while the repressed, restrained child holds on to childishness more tenaciously.

Why should this be so? Perhaps this is yet another proof that so-called childish behavior during the years after early childhood is not necessarily natural to children but is instead a reaction to cultural circumstances that have been, until quite recently, a universal part of childhood (though not for migrant farm-worker children, nor for the boys and girls in the dark Satanic mills). These circumstances require that children repress certain instincts and that they suppress their sexuality completely, in conformance with codes of behavior emphasizing obedience and submission to adults. Perhaps those treasured manifestations of children's joyful innocence are actually compensatory outlets to counteract society-induced repressions, a sort of let-loose-from-the-chains reaction, as when a puppy taken off the leash tears about and plays wildly and foolishly. This is not to deny that children are endowed with special drives of curiosity or playfulness —play, we have come to understand, defines much of the work of childhood—but rather to suggest that these drives are strengthened and allowed full release when the child is held back in other ways and that period of life known as childhood is prolonged.

THIRTEEN

THE MEANING OF CHILDHOOD

MAKING UP FOR THE LOSS

Here is a puzzle. According to widely accepted theories of modern psychology, children cannot grow up successfully without the steady care and protection of loving parents. But what about children of past eras, the children of medieval times, for instance, who were cast out into the world unprotected at an early age? Did they all grow up to be warped, affectless creatures, as our current understanding would lead us to believe, incapable of love and empathy, mindlessly clobbering old ladies on the head? Or could it be that these assumptions, based as they are largely on Freud's observations of the parent-child relations that obtained in his particular society, do not universally hold true for children of differently structured societies?

Perhaps, as we suspect, if the basic security children *do* universally need is not provided by a mother and father within a cozy nuclear family, there are other ways for them to find emotional support and protection. We speculate that in medieval times a network of kinfolk or neighbors took on a more protective role towards the free-floating children in their community than adults assume today towards children who are not their own. In such a way, perhaps, children long ago managed to grow up emotionally uncrippled in spite of the fact that their immediate family did not seem to feel obliged to take special care of them.

What about the increasing number of children today who grow up without the security of an unbroken family and the special, undivided protection of a parental caretaker during the childhood years? Is some compensatory source of gratification available for children who are being raised in single-parent households, or in homes with both parents fully employed, or in those families who simply no longer believe that protection is good for children and take a preparatory stance in their child rearing? Might children not, indeed, be better off without that intense parent-child bond that causes all those terrible conflicts Freud described?

We know that in recent years certain extrafamilial services for children *have* begun to spring up, directed specifically at problems caused by divorce and new parental employment patterns. Schools and communities *have* begun to provide counseling, guidance, and even a strange sort of affection for many children whose families no longer meet their basic needs. Indeed, schools have become so important a family substitute these days that graduation ceremonies are often scenes of true grief and mourning, with the departing students displaying the sort of separation anxiety that in former times accompanied a child's leavetaking from home and parents.

There is also reason to believe that great numbers of children today are seeking a new sort of gratification and support from another readily available source: their peers. Of course, children have long formed special ties with their age-mates. But there are fundamental differences between the bonds formed in the protective past and the peer relations among children today; while the friendships of earlier eras sought to build new strengths, those of today are often forged out of shared weaknesses.

The peer group of the past, with its fearful "peer pressure" to which parents used to ascribe so many of their difficulties with their teenage children, was a clear-cut manifestation of the adolescent's rebellion against parental authority. In the company of their peers children who had heretofore been protected from hardship and danger struck out for separation and independence; only thus could they pave the way for true autonomy. But the clinging together of little bands of children that we see so often today has a different aspect. For one thing, peer banding sets in far earlier. Until ten or fifteen years ago the family was all-important during the years before adolescence, and family-centered activities dominated children's social life well into their teen years. Today many parents report that their children begin to turn against family-centered activities as early as fifth or sixth grade, preferring suddenly to spend their time with small groups of friends.

While the teenagers of the past sought the company of their peers for testing behavior, for taking risks, driving too fast, breaking the rules, and, of course, testing their sexual powers, all activities designed to undermine the cozy stability and security of their protected lives, it may be that very stability and security that today's eleven-, twelve-, and thirteen-year-olds are seeking in each other's company as they spend their afternoons or evenings "turning on" with marijuana, listening to rock music, and "making out." There is something needy about their precocious sexual relations; often, some have observed, their behavior has an oddly unsexual quality, as if they were searching for a closeness and affection with each other that children their age were once wont to find with their parents. And by the same token, the dreamy hours they spend together getting stoned is a far cry from the endless talking, planning, debating, boasting, complaining, and just plain fooling around that the peer group of yore used to engage in. Rather, getting "buzzed" together seems to represent an attempt to recapture a carefree, passive state of dependence, a feeling of irresponsibility and safety—a childhood, in short, that they have had to give up early.

Children's new peer bonds are not only with their age-mates but with their traditional rivals: siblings. In today's changing family scene, brothers and sisters not infrequently lend each other the help and protection they are failing to receive from their parents. Mel Roman, a professor of psychiatry at Albert Einstein College who has studied children of divorce, believes that during a marital crisis the siblings form the most important support system. "The breakup inevitably draws the kids together," he says, noting that the older siblings often take on an openly parental role towards their younger brothers and sisters. This affords them a certain adult gratification while providing the younger ones with the extra attention and care that they crave.[1]

How different such a situation is from the traditional sibling struggle within the intact family. There, the classic Freudian "sibling rivalry" for the exclusive love of the parents with whom the children have formed so close and intense an attachment precludes any real bonding between brothers and sisters until long after all the parent-child conflicts are resolved. Anna Freud herself pointed out the connection between the dynamics of sibling rivalry and the child's social situation when she observed:

> The jealousy between brothers and sisters is much less when the relations to the mother are not so close. In working-class families, where the mother is able to devote far less care to her children, the loss of tenderness at the birth of younger children is correspondingly less. Hence there is to be found among working-class children much more love and sympathy than in middle-class families. In the latter each child sees in the other children . . . a rival for a very real possession, and accordingly hatred and jealousy, open or hidden, dominate the relations between brothers and sisters.[2]

Even pets are invoked today as an accommodation to a new style of parent-child relations, much as the peer group seems to serve. As Jane Brody writes in the *New York Times*, "In this age when both parents are often at work when children come home from school, pets offer children a dependable 'welcome home' and a feeling of security."[3]

If friends and siblings and even pets have stepped into the breach these days, to serve as replacements or at least as compensations for the care and close bonding between parents and children that we once considered a *sine qua non* for emotional health, might we not breathe a sigh of relief and look upon today's situation with greater optimism? There is after all some evidence to support the notion that peer relations *may*, under certain circumstances, substitute for the intimate parent-child bond of traditional, protective families. In his study of child rearing on an Israeli kibbutz, Bruno Bettelheim proposed that for those communally reared children just such a thing occurs. In the place of an intimate parent-child bond, Bettelheim suggests, the kibbutz children substitute a stable, deep, and dependable attachment to a small group of other children; this relationship provides them with the emotional security they require.[4]

But the kibbutz is a special environment, a simplified, rural, homogeneous enclave of voluntary devotees, as stable and self-sufficient a setup as the feudal village may have been. Perhaps under such circumstances children may fulfill each other's deep needs. But outside such protected environs the modern world is too unstable, too complex, too dangerous for children to wing it on their own, or simply with the help of other immature organisms like themselves.

Man is an adaptive animal, and as children congregate in their little bands today they are, indeed, adapting to their extraordinarily vulnerable situation by seeking each other's company. But like those children who suffer from pica, a severe iron-deficiency disease that causes them to compulsively consume quantities of dirt, sand, or clay, today's children are not finding true nourishment in their compensatory activities. The consequences of their sexual involvements are often disastrous as they discover they cannot provide each other the emotional security they crave, and they sometimes find themselves with an unwanted pregnancy as well. Their dependence on drugs or alcohol does not afford them the true safety and insouciance that they seek; indeed, it often thrusts them into a more perilous world than the one they are fleeing. Perhaps siblings, forced to drop their former childhood rivalry, do form stronger bonds today as they struggle with their common unhappiness, but it is hard to suppose that these will compensate for the loss of security, of trust, of that unselfconscious enjoyment of life that was once considered the right of every child.

CHILDREN'S LIBERATION

It might seem to some that minimizing the gap between childhood and adulthood and treating children with greater equality represents a step up for them, a liberation from a semi-enslaved state into one in which they are endowed with rights just like adults. But treating a child in an equal way, as if he were another adult, contradicts the underlying social realities of the parent-child relationship and ignores the innate, developmental differences that exist between the two. The new concept of the child as equal and the new integration of children into adult life has helped bring about a gradual but certain erosion of those boundaries that once separated the world of children from the world of adults, boundaries that allowed adults to treat children differently than they treated other adults because they understood that children *are* different. Those boundaries prevented children from behaving freely because it was understood that the behavior children will naturally manifest, if allowed equal rights, will *not* resemble adult behavior and will frequently interfere with the freedom of adults to conduct their lives properly.

The particular difficulties that arise when the difference between children and adults is denied were observed in an extreme form by some of the idealistic student activists of the 1960s after they married and began to cope with the problems of parenthood. A father of three sons, today a director of a human rights organization, was such a parent. He tells of the tension between his belief in children's rights and the daily realities of parenthood:

"When we started out as parents in the early seventies, we believed very strongly that our children should be free and should have rights equal to any other human beings. By the time the children were old enough to understand words, we began spelling out their freedom to them, the fact that they didn't *have* to do what we say just because we're bigger and stronger, that they were entitled to their own opinions and desires. But it really worked disastrously. I'd say to them 'I want you to go outside now,' because I had work to do and I wanted them to go out and play, but they'd say, 'We don't have to. You said you're not going to tell us what to do.' Or they'd come up and say, 'I want to sit on your lap now,' and I'd say, 'You'll have to wait until I finish this job,' and they'd say, 'No, I want to sit in your lap and I'm *going* to whether you want me to or not!' We realized pretty soon that giving them absolute freedom was not enough, that you had to make them understand that people's rights can infringe on each other. And we soon realized that such an understanding was much too complicated for them. They just weren't old enough to be able to restrain themselves on their own. We came to see that children simply need the security of authority, even though I still believe that adults shouldn't operate that way."

The knowledge that a child is unable to understand the complex rules of human behavior, that he does not know that freedom must be limited by a respect for the rights of others—for instance, that there are rules of communication which require people to talk in turn and to give others a chance to express themselves fully—must lead to the establishment of special rules for children that prevent them from interfering with adult rights. Only temporary amnesia based either on idealistic beliefs in equality or, more commonly today, on unfamiliarity with the realities of childhood because parents are busy or distracted, would cause them to allow a child to be an equal partner in ordinary social relations in the adult world, or to suppose that the child will somehow rise to the occasion and not be annoying, dominating, obstreperous, demanding, and generally as self-centered as it is perfectly natural for a child to be at that stage of development. In a way the removal of the traditional boundaries between children and adults may have an opposite effect from the children's-rights goal, delaying rather than facilitating that very liberation the hopeful activists of the sixties dreamed of achieving for their children. For in reality, granting children equality often deprives them of the safety and security that can be enjoyed only in a structured world, one in which adults are adults taking care of children, while children are children, dependent upon and consequently unequal to adults.

In an article on children's rights, Federal Judge Mary Kohler hailed "the right to be a child during childhood," and emphasized that one of the impediments to the achievement of this "inalienable" right is the "too early forcing of choices" upon children.[5] The right to be a child may well have seemed inalienable ten or fifteen years ago, when the article was published. Today parents are inclined to prepare children for the future by precisely that "forcing of choices." The very concept of this happening "too early" is disappearing.

THE POVERTY OF CHILDHOOD

There are those who see childhood as a form of deprivation. Critic Helen Vendler, for instance, refers to "the poverty of every child's restricted life" as she describes "the passage from a sequestered childhood to a forcibly socialized adulthood."[6] The implication of the word "poverty" in conjunction with the idea of a "sequestered" childhood is this: were the child to be offered the full wealth of experience that is available to the adult, he would be enriched by it. Because he is protected from it, however, the child must be seen as poor and incompleted. Yet there is reason to think that this is a misguided sentiment.

Part of that wealth from which children were once sequestered was a questionable enrichment: the knowledge of evil, violence, human helplessness, futility, injustice, misery, death. Today, as parents struggle for economic survival and search for sexual fulfillment, as they divorce, remarry, work out their primitive conflicts with their shrinks, rail against political corruption, agonize over depleting natural resources and ecological destruction, tremble at the nuclear threat, they no longer sequester their children from knowledge of and involvement in these complex affairs. It is not always because they are no longer capable of hiding these difficult subjects, but also because they believe it is better to prepare children than to protect them.

Those who believe that to protect children is to impoverish them, who feel therefore that it is preferable to allow children free entry into every sort of adult experience, are making a crucial assumption: that children have the same capacity as adults to assimilate and utilize knowledge and experience. There are many who take issue with such an assumption.

Annie Herman, an early-childhood expert, explicitly disagrees with such a viewpoint. Indeed, she connects some of the problems that seem almost to define today's youth with just this failure to differentiate children's needs from those of adults:

"Trying to do away with the discrepancies between children and adults is more prevalent in America than in Europe. We rather feel it is helping to promote equality and democracy to treat children as equal, and for this reason we feel obliged to share all our adult knowledge with them. But it's like feeding a two-day-old child with a delicious steak. We justify our action by saying that we love to eat steak and therefore it's only fair to give it to our child. But the child has no teeth, and cannot eat the steak. He chokes on it.

"We want our children to know very soon that we are not as wonderful as they think. We feel it is unfair, undemocratic somehow, to let children have false illusions about adult omnipotence. So instead of letting the child believe parents are wise and powerful, that adults will always come to the rescue in time of need, we tell our children, 'Oh, we're just like you. We have faults and weaknesses.' But the child has his own timetable of development and cannot manage to absorb the realities of adult life when they are foisted on him prematurely."

Moreover, Dr. Herman continues, "innocence, once considered the right of children, may be seen as simply the absence of weight and burden. Maturity, meanwhile, may be defined as the capacity to carry a burden successfully. But if you are given the heavy burden of knowledge before you have the capacity to deal with it—and knowledge *is* burdensome, because it requires mental and psychological work to deal with it—the results may be those very signs they observe in their children which are distressing parents and teachers today: confusion, fear, feelings of incompetence. Children grow up not really able to deal with difficulties, seeking avenues of escape, and they learn that the best way to deal with problems is to escape, through drugs or drink or whatever."[7]

Because of the precocious knowledge, the worldly savoir-faire, the independence, the assertiveness, the confident sense of equality in communicating with adults that characterize so many children today—especially, it appears, those who have had to "grow up faster" because their mother and father have divorced or are both absorbed in their careers—it is easy to get the impression that children are also more mature these days. Indeed, the child growing up under more protective, old-fashioned circumstances may seem more "bratty," more "spoiled," more demanding than the hardy, self-sufficient child of absent parents. But whether the greatest level of maturity is reached when one has a shorter rather than a longer period of dependence and protection is the great unanswered question. Based on the evidence of contemporary children, it appears that while a certain level of sophistication and suavity is achieved when a child is forced to take care of himself much of the time, it is not at all the same thing as maturity. As the child grows older, true maturity, defined by an ability to share, to empathize, to sacrifice, to be generous, to love unselfishly, and to nurture and care for children of his own, may prove elusive, and in its place attention seeking and narcissism become the characteristics that define his adult life.

A thirteen-year-old girl whose parents divorced when she was nine points out the connection between an unprotected childhood and difficulties achieving maturity: "When my parents split, things were a terrible mess. They were too upset and too involved in their own things to pay much attention to me, and I guess in a lot of ways I had to bring myself up. I really did grow up very fast, faster than a lot of kids. But actually this didn't make me end up more mature than my friends. If anything, it worked the other way. I need a lot of attention, a lot of talking things out—really, a lot more than most of my friends who grew up more slowly."

Psychoanalyst Peter Neubauer adds a warning that reverberates with particular resonance in a time of increasing narcissism: "Children who are pushed into adult experience do not become precociously mature. On the contrary, they cling to childhood longer, perhaps all their lives."[8]

The poverty of childhood, we begin to suspect, is a misleading concept. While those children whose childhoods are enriched by a bounty of adult experiences end up the poorer for it, those "poor," protected children have received a treasure in disguise—one, however, that will reveal itself only when they have grown up. As Annie Herman explains: "The child *needs* to feel dependent on the adult, has a *right* to this feeling. If the adult is just like the child after all, then the child can't really depend on him. And yet that stage of childhood when children believe in parental omnipotence helps develop a basic, life-giving trust, a trust that carries with it half of life's enjoyment long after childhood has ended."[9]

THE PURPOSE OF CHILDHOOD

Why do creation myths in so many cultures begin with a paradise so soon to be lost? Why does the story not start right off with the original couple discovering human existence to be the sort of mixed bag of happiness and sorrow that life on earth was in the beginning and is now and probably ever shall be? Perhaps because the makers of the myths understood that human life does indeed begin in a Garden of Eden of sorts, where every need is taken care of and every desire fulfilled—childhood. And yet it is a finite paradise, which must end when the child grows up.

But more than describing a reality—that human life begins with childhood—the major creation myth of our culture, the story of Adam and Eve and their expulsion from the Garden of Eden, contains within it an illumination of the meaning of childhood and its purpose in human life. That the Garden of Eden tale is a metaphor not only for the Childhood of Mankind at its creation but for the childhood of individual men and women is supported by a close examination of the story itself. Each detail of the spare but densely meaningful tale may be related to an aspect of childhood.

Consider the sole condition on which Adam and Eve's term in Paradise depends: it is not that they be good, or that they work hard, or that they be clever, the usual requirements for success in fairy tales or in real life. It is simply that they remain innocent: "Of the tree of knowledge of good and evil, thou shalt not eat of it" is their only injunction from the Lord. As long as they desist from sampling the forbidden fruit, they may remain in the happy Garden, protected from all harm, free of all care. Just so, children are loved and nourished whether or not they behave well or pick up their toys or get A's on their report cards. But their optimal care is as contingent on their childlike innocence as the first Man and Woman's stay in Eden was contingent on theirs. Once children are allowed to discover the complex secrets of the adult world, their days in Paradise are numbered; the dependable protection they once enjoyed is soon transformed into a hardening process that is to prepare them for a difficult life.

What exactly happened when Adam and Eve took the fatal step and ate the forbidden apple? What gave them away? Oddly enough, though it was the fruit of the Tree of Knowledge they had ingested, it did not cause them suddenly to exhibit great wisdom, to declaim learned aphorisms or spout algebraic formulas or engage in pithy dialectics. A simple thing betrayed them: they became self-conscious. Though they were naked from the moment of their creation in Paradise, in their original innocence they had been completely unashamed. Now they tried to hide their nakedness from the Lord. "Who told thee that thou wast naked?" the Lord asked, knowing immediately that they had disobeyed. It was their very awareness of being naked that revealed a new consciousness and defined the end of their innocence.

Children, too, lose that natural and unselfconscious ability to enjoy life directly as they learn early the bewildering secrets of the adult world. In biological terms, however, that childlike unawareness of self is one of those neotenic traits specific to the young and programmed to elicit protectiveness from adults. Childhood may thus remain safe and secure—in a word, Paradise.

Why, in fact, did Adam and Eve have to pass through that perfectly innocent and happy state on their way to fulfill their human destiny? Did that period of innocence and safety serve a purpose in their post-Edenic existence? And what, by the same token, might a happy and protected childhood provide for humans in their later life? Clearly, everyone has a childhood of some sort. But for some it is longer than for others, and for some it is close to a heaven. Does it make a great difference, as the myth suggests?

It is in the nature of that particular unselfconsciousness preceding the Fall that we must seek the first great purpose of childhood. For if we consider that ineffable part of Man which often allows him to endure the bitter sufferings that follow his Fall and to live with the unbearable knowledge of his own mortality—the mysterious creative, artistic drive—we may see that its wellsprings lie within that special sensibility of childhood.

Many have observed that certain artists have a rare ability to recapture the spontaneous, fresh way of experiencing life that children enjoy. A century ago the German poet and playwright Schiller defined such artists as "naïve"—those who produce their art directly from their own being, without ratiocination or self-analysis. Such artists are as harmoniously integrated with their art as children are in their direct involvement with life. Schiller compared these with a different artistic sensibility that he called "sentimental." This other sort of artist, in Schiller's dichotomy, can only look at that harmony between sense and thinking as an ideal. Self-consciously, such artists search to recapture that vanished world that was once part of them and strive to re-create it in their imagination. The first type of artist, who has somehow remained a child even as an adult, is rare indeed.

Most adults have access to their childhood experience only through that second, indirect means. But the "naïve" and the "sentimental" forms of artistic expression have a common ground that unites them: each is informed by the special consciousness of childhood. If childhood is early infiltrated—contaminated, one might go so far as to say —by adult ways of thinking and behaving, there is a danger that a loss will be felt by generations to come whose artistic reserves will be low, or perhaps nonexistent.

But why prolong childhood? Perhaps even a brief spell in Paradise will provide enough inspiration for future Shakespeares and Homers. The story of Adam and Eve provides yet another clue to yet another purpose of childhood. We observe an odd exception to the carefree and irresponsible life the original couple were given to live in the Garden of Eden: Adam was assigned a particular task, that of giving a name to every living creature in the newly created world, "to all cattle, and to the fowl of the air, and to every beast of the field." A sizable job, when you stop to think of it. But in the Biblical story this taxonomic enterprise is clearly distinguished from the dangerous understanding that resides in the Tree of Knowledge. That alone is forbidden; other forms of knowledge, evidently, are encouraged.

Children too have a task of childhood, not so unlike Adam's task: to systematically accumulate information, to learn, to go to school. Though they must not eat of the Tree of Knowledge if they are to remain children, this other sort of intellectual nourishment is necessary.

We have seen that in other historical times and in other cultures childhood ended far earlier than it does in modern times. But those were simpler times, the childhood of civilization, in a sense. The adults of the Middle Ages, it appears, were themselves more childlike in their ways of thinking and behaving than adults are today, and perhaps more childlike than not a few of today's children. But the more highly developed the species becomes and the more complex the civilization, the lengthier a childhood is required. There is just that much more learning to assimilate. And childhood *is* that time when the human organism has the leisure to lay a solid intellectual foundation upon which it may in later years build a structure of some sort, one that might possibly have significance for the species as a whole. The long childhood hours, if childhood remains an Eden of stability and safety, may be occupied by the slow, methodical accumulation of cultural material culled from the great efforts of thinkers of the past. Like Adam, that original Linnaeus, children can apply themselves to an understanding of all living creatures, their names, their histories, their biology and chemistry. Steadily, under the conditions of dependence with all questions of survival taken care of by others, children may learn how to learn.

The final purpose of childhood is exemplified by the very inevitability of the Fall itself, in chapter 3 of Genesis. Although Adam and Eve are censured for their weakness in giving way to temptation and are held responsible for all the sufferings that make human life so far from paradisiacal, there was in fact a grand purpose to their eating of the fruit of knowledge. They *had* to leave Paradise, to grow up in another sense, in order to start the human race. "And Adam knew his wife; and she conceived, and bare Cain," begins the next chapter of the story, after the expulsion from Eden. The fateful primal pair made their trade-off, losing blissful dependence to gain wisdom and sexual maturity for a reason: the future of humankind depended on it.

Like Adam and Eve, each child must lose his place in Paradise to grow up. Each child must learn the bitter and yet thrilling secrets of adulthood, must face the dangers of the world of capricious natural phenomena and unpredictable human relations, and confront the terrors of mortality, in order to survive as an adult, to live independently, to fulfill his particular mission on the earth, whatever it might be. And above all, to become a successful parent, thus continuing the task of Adam and Eve. But it is in the carrying out of that very task that the deepest purpose of childhood lies. Only through the lengthy experience of being a child, of being dependent, of being totally protected and nurtured by loving parents, does the child gain the ability to be a successful, protective, nurturing parent himself.

The connection between one's childhood and one's subsequent outcome as an adult has been demonstrated again and again by negative studies: a miserable childhood leads to a troubled adulthood. Battered children grow up to become battering parents. The connection between a long, happy childhood and a rich, fulfilled adulthood, between the quality of one's childhood and one's ability to be a good, loving parent, is harder to pin down. Nevertheless we have our myths of Paradise to teach us the truth about childhood. There must be an Eden at the beginning, just as there is in every creation myth. The future of humankind still depends on it.

*T*HE NEW MIDDLE AGES

*T*oday, after several centuries of childhood as an estate carefully separated from adulthood, it begins to appear that we are returning to a long-ago pattern of undifferentiation—a New Middle Ages, we might call it.

There is little doubt that since the 1960s children have come to resemble adults more closely than they have done for centuries. In the clothes they wear, the language they use, and the things they know, in all aspects of their daily behavior, children today seem less childlike.

Consider the change that has overtaken children's leisure time. Centuries ago, children and adults played games together in the streets and sang songs and listened to stories together indoors. In later times, children and adults went off in divergent directions. Today, in the New Middle Ages, children read books about prostitution and see movies about adult marital problems. They listen to music with a strong sexual beat. And adults and children are again united in their most important leisure-time deployment. No longer do kids play while adults engage in more grown-up activities: young and old alike these days spend most of their free time watching television.

Consider the complex code of manners that developed slowly over the centuries, serving to separate children's behavior sharply from adults'. There is no law decreeing that what develops slowly cannot be "undeveloped" quickly, perhaps even within a few decades. The shame and revulsion that it took civilized folks so long to acquire seem to have taken them only a single generation to loosen and in some cases slough off entirely. A new openness prevails. Today we learn from our therapists to feel more ashamed of our repressions than of "letting it all hang out." In the New Middle Ages parents no longer have dinner alone by candlelight while children eat in the nursery, learning the proper way to use their forks and knives. Now the whole family can go out and eat with their fingers at the Kentucky Fried Chicken place down the street.

Consider the demise of sexual innocence among children. We know that the casual integration of children into adult society in the Middle Ages included few sexual prohibitions. Today's nine- and ten-year-olds watch pornographic movies on cable TV, casually discourse about oral sex and sadomasochism, and not infrequently find themselves involved in their own parents' complicated sex lives, if not as actual observers or participants, at least as advisers, friendly commentators, and intermediaries. Yet another portent of the New Middle Ages.

Consider that curious medieval convention of sending children away from home at an early age to live in other people's houses. Until as late as the eighteenth century, children as young as seven years old were sent off for training to households similar to their own. At the same time that people sent their own children away, they took other people's children into their own homes. In this way the primary ties between parents and children were broken early. According to our current understanding of child psychology, such a deprivation and loss would serve to make children more docile and malleable, less exuberant and childlike. Had they remained at home their natural psychological vigor, their healthy egocentrism, might have made them resist their parents' demands for work and services, just as children today frequently go to great lengths to avoid doing any work around the house.

Today too the primary ties are broken early for great numbers of children. Now, instead of sending the children away, it is the parents who go away, their exits precipitated by separation, divorce, or work requirements. The consequences for the children, however, are similar to those that accompanied the child departures of old: depression, a loss of vigor, and the end of childhood as a period of carefree dependence.

Consider, finally, the recent change in the popular iconography of childhood—that is, the way children are represented in movies and books and especially in television programs and commercials. Just as on television today we see children transformed by make-up, clothing, facial expressions, and gestures (sexually suggestive dancing, for instance) into pseudo-adults, so we may begin to understand the strange distortion of children in medieval paintings and drawings that made them look like small, dwarflike adults rather than children. The recognition of childhood as a separate and different state from adulthood did not then, and does not today, suit the inner purposes of society.

It has become fashionable to idealize the distant past, to suppose that when children were integrated into society they were somehow better off. Yet critics of the current nostalgia point out evidence of widespread sexual exploitation, neglect, and abuse of children in the medieval period. Similarly, as we make the transition from an era in which children were separated and protected from adult hardships to one in which they are once again incorporated early into a more casual and undifferentiated society, we cannot fail to observe that child abuse and child exploitation are once again on the increase and that the lives of great numbers of children have not improved but instead have worsened.

It may indeed prove that children have become increasingly useful to adults in modern society as their roles have changed from innocent, dependent, "special" creatures to secret and not-so-secret sharers of adult life's inevitable burdens. But from the viewpoint of children themselves, whether the strengths they may derive from their earlier preparation for adulthood will compensate for the loss of that carefree childhood that people once believed children deserve and require remains in doubt. But there is no doubt that childhood is harder today. As a fifteen-year-old girl who looks back on a past that included a parental divorce, experimentation with marijuana from sixth grade on, and a troubling experience with sex in eighth grade remarked: "All the kids I see are in a rush to grow up, and I don't blame them. I don't think childhood is a golden age at all. I wouldn't want to be a child again."

This is not to suggest that childhood in the bygone Age of Protection was a continuously blessed, happy state. Rare indeed was the child who did not experience jealousy or terror or shame or anger or any of the other myriad forms of human misery at some time during the childhood years. In his book *Growing Up*, for example, journalist Russell Baker describes his childhood during the Depression years, darkened by poverty, marital discord, illness, and death. And yet he is able to write: "The occasional outbursts of passion that flickered across my childhood were like summer storms. The sky clouded suddenly, thunder rumbled, lightning flashed and I trembled a few moments, then just as swiftly the sky turned blue again and I was basking contentedly again in the peace of innocence."[1] It is not by chance that when Baker paints a scene to describe the overriding mood of his childhood days he peoples it with adults sitting on a porch, rocking and pronouncing beliefs such as "Children should be seen and not heard," interrupting their gossip with reminders that "Little pitchers have big ears." For it was not the complete absence of unhappiness in those early years that allowed him to look back on his childhood as an island of peace and innocence. It was the secure certainty that he was a child and that adults were adults, and that in spite of the wretchedness he might glimpse in their world he could still remain, in his different state, untouched by it. This is the essence of adult protectiveness: transmitting to children the sense that they are separate and special and under the adults' careful supervision. This understanding allowed children of the past, even those growing up a mere ten or fifteen years ago, to enjoy the simple pleasures of childhood—of play, imagination, curiosity, and pursuit of adventure —in the most adverse circumstances.

Can the boundaries between adulthood and childhood be once again restored? Can parents today, who sense uneasily that something is missing, try to re-create the different sort of childhood that they themselves once enjoyed? In an Age of Preparation, can individual parents hope to buck the tide and try to bring their children up protectively?

The social processes that helped bring about children's new integration into adult life—changes in family stability, most notably, together with women's liberation and the proliferation of television as a dominant part of children's lives—cannot be reversed. We will never return to the old-style family with the bread-earning father and the childlike, stay-at-home mother minding the house and kids. Nor would we desire such a step backward. The liberation movement has brought a new maturity and independence to women, forcing them, sometimes against their deepest instincts, to seek to fulfill a greater potential than they had understood in the past. The hope of a simple turning of the tide is an unrealistic and indeed a retrogressive one. Nevertheless, while social change cannot be reversed, perhaps it can be modified and made to work better for families.

Perhaps an understanding of the irreversible consequences of family breakdown on children may cause men and women to readjust some of their original goals for marriage. If their objectives are primarily self-fulfillment, sexual excitement, a deeply gratifying adult relationship, then it might be advisable for them to think twice about embarking on a family in the first place. The thought of a family mainly as a source of fulfillment and gratification for the marriage partners does not bode well for children's future. Parents need to understand that the successful raising of a family requires a greater focus on the well-being of the children and that they must sacrifice some of their own ambitions, desires, and strivings for personal happiness if the children are to grow up well. It may be the future holds the possibility of a variety of partnerships for men and women, only some of which will be seen as conducive to the raising of children.

Perhaps an understanding that early childhood is not the only important stage of childhood, that the middle years are equally important, may lead parents to compromise their career and social ambitions and devote more time and attention, more care and supervision, to their post-toddler children, capable and unchildlike though they may seem. As child-development specialist Annie Herman proposes, the early childhood years may not necessarily be the most crucial ones, in spite of the orthodox view that the personality is formed during those years. "There is a certain resilience in early childhood," she explains, "but this resilience slowly disappears. When you are resilient you bounce back. Thus young children can recover from physical and mental trauma quickly and can put things aside and turn to other things. But as they grow older their resilience is diminished. At this point the child becomes far more vulnerable to outside experience. Now the child can suffer permanent damage."

Perhaps an understanding of the importance of play in children's lives, not only to the child directly as a source of a particular kind of satisfaction but as an activity that helps define the child as a childlike creature, thus promoting more protective treatment by adults, will provoke parents to take a stronger stand in controlling their children's television viewing, television being the single great replacement of play among today's children.

Perhaps an understanding that children and adults are *not* equal, and that children do not prosper when treated as equal, will encourage parents to take a more authoritative—authoritative, not authoritarian—position in the family.

Perhaps the recognition that a highly complicated civilization cannot afford to shorten the period of nurture and protection of its immature members will restore a real childhood to the children of coming generations.

NOTES

INTRODUCTION. SOMETHING HAS HAPPENED

1. "Parents Pages," *National Lampoon,* Kids Issue, June 1979.
2. Advertisement for Flare Books (Avon imprint) in *Publishers Weekly,* March 13, 1981.

CHAPTER ONE. OUT-OF-CONTROL PARENTS

1. Alison Lurie, *The War Between the Tates* (New York: Random House, 1974), pp. 6–7.
2. Betty Wason, *Ellen: A Mother's Story of Her Runaway Daughter* (New York: Readers Digest Press, 1976), p. 162.
3. Michael Satchell, "Head Shops: Gateway to the Drug Scene," *Parade,* June 15, 1980.
4. Frank J. Furstenberg et al., eds., *Teenage Sexuality, Pregnancy and Childbearing* (Philadelphia: University of Pennsylvania Press, 1980).
5. Melvin Zelnick and John F. Kantner, "Sexual Activity, Contraceptive Use, and Pregnancy Among Metropolitan Area Teenagers, 1971–1979," *Family Planning Perspectives* 12 (September–October 1980).
6. John Bowlby, *Child Care and the Growth of Love,* 2nd ed. (New York: Penguin Books, 1965).
7. Joseph McVicker Hunt, *Intelligence and Experience* (New York: Ronald Press, 1961). Benjamin S. Bloom, *Stability and Change in Human Characteristics* (New York: John Wiley, 1964). Harry F. Harlow and Margaret K. Harlow, "Social Deprivation in Monkeys," *Scientific American* 207 (1962). Christopher Jencks et al., *Inequality: A Reassessment of the Effect of Family and Schooling in America* (New York: Basic Books, 1972).
8. Elizabeth Brynner, "The New Parental Push Against Marijuana," *New York Times Magazine,* February 10, 1980.
9. John Demos, "The American Family in Past Time," in Arlene Skolnick

and Jerome Skolnick, eds., *Family in Transition*, 2nd ed. (Boston: Little, Brown, 1977), pp. 63–64.

10. Joseph Heller, *Something Happened* (New York: Alfred A. Knopf, 1974), pp. 178–79.
11. Richard A. Hawley, *Some Unsettling Thoughts About Settling In with Pot*, University School Press Occasional Paper, 1978, p. 18.
12. *Families Anonymous Credo*, distributed by Families Anonymous Inc., P.O. Box 344, Torrance, California 90501.
13. See Marie Winn, *The Plug-In Drug: Television, Children and the Family* (New York: Viking Press, 1977).

CHAPTER TWO. THE NEW EQUALITY

1. Phillip Lopate, in a personal interview with the author.
2. Henry T. Harbin, M.D., and Dennis J. Madden, Ph.D., "Battered Parents: A New Syndrome," *American Journal of Psychiatry* 136 (October 1979).

CHAPTER THREE. THE END OF SECRECY

1. Joyce Maynard, "Coming of Age with Judy Blume," *New York Times Magazine*, December 3, 1978.
2. Summary of Fran Arrick, *Steffie Can't Come Out to Play* (Scarsdale, N.Y.: Bradbury Press, 1978).
3. John Donovan, *I'll Get There, It Better Be Worth the Trip* (New York: Harper & Row, 1969).
4. Al Feldstein, in a personal interview with the author, 1981.
5. Richard Heffner, in a personal interview with the author.
6. For a full description of this experiment, see Phillip Lopate, "Chekhov for Children," *Teachers and Writers Magazine* 11 (Winter 1979).
7. John Rothchild, *The Children of the Counterculture* (New York: Doubleday, 1976).
8. Anna Freud, *Psychoanalysis for Teachers and Parents* (New York: W. W. Norton, 1979), p. 37.
9. Katharine Rees and Dr. Paulina F. Kernberg, in personal interviews with the author.

CHAPTER FOUR. THE END OF PLAY

1. *Current Population Reports* (Washington, D.C.: Bureau of the Census, 1980).

CHAPTER FIVE. CHILDHOOD OF THE PAST

1. Philippe Ariès, *Centuries of Childhood: A Social History of Family Life,* trans. Robert Baldick (New York: Alfred A. Knopf, 1962).
2. Emmanuel Le Roy Ladurie, *Montaillou: The Promised Land of Error,* trans. Barbara Bray (New York: Vintage Books, 1979).
3. Norbert Elias, *The Civilizing Process,* vol. 1, *The History of Manners,* trans. Edmund Jephcott (New York: Pantheon Books, 1982), pp. 129–31, 140.

CHAPTER SIX. NEW-ERA CHILD REARING

1. A. Freud, *Psychoanalysis for Teachers and Parents,* p. 41.
2. Erich Fromm, *Greatness and Limitations of Freud's Thought* (New York: Harper & Row, 1980).
3. Talcott Parsons, "The Social Structure of the Family," in Ruth Nanda Anshen, ed., *The Family: Its Function and Destiny* (New York: Harper & Row, 1949).
4. Benjamin M. Spock, *The Common Sense Book of Baby and Child Care* (New York: Duell, Sloan & Pearce, 1949). Revised edition: *Baby and Child Care* (New York: Pocket Books, 1968), p. 338.
5. Selma Fraiberg, *The Magic Years* (New York: Charles Scribner's Sons, 1959). The passages quoted are from pp. 246–50, 253, and 250–51.
6. John Demos, "Infancy and Childhood in the Plymouth Colony," in Michael Gordon, ed., *The American Family in Socio-Historical Perspective* (New York: St. Martin's Press, 1973).
7. Erik Erikson, *Childhood and Society* (New York: W. W. Norton, 1963).

CHAPTER SEVEN. THE END OF SYMBIOSIS

1. Quoted by Barbara Welter in "The Cult of True Womanhood," in Gordon, ed., *American Family in Socio-Historical Perspective,* p. 318.
2. Quoted by Welter in "Cult of True Womanhood," p. 325.
3. *Trends in Child Care Arrangements of Working Mothers,* Current Population Reports Special Studies (Washington, D.C.: Bureau of the Census, August 1982).

CHAPTER EIGHT. THE END OF MARRIAGE

1. Heather L. Ross and Isabel V. Sawhill, *Time of Transition: The Growth of Families Headed by Women* (Washington, D.C.: Urban Institute, 1975).

2. *Marital Status and Living Arrangements: March 1981* (Washington, D.C.: Bureau of the Census, July 1982).
3. Quoted in "The Children of Divorce," *Newsweek*, February 11, 1980.
4. Dr. Paulina F. Kernberg, in a personal interview with the author.
5. Katharine Rees, in a personal interview with the author.
6. Judy Glass, "Runaways: Why They Go," *New York Times*, August 30, 1981.
7. David Finkelhor, *Parents, Children and Child Sexual Abuse: Three Reports from a Boston Survey*, The Family Violence Research Project, University of New Hampshire in Durham, 1983.
8. Gary Small and Armand M. Nichols, "Mass Hysteria Among Schoolchildren: Early Loss as a Predisposing Factor," *Archives of General Psychiatry* 39 (June 1982).
9. Dr. Peter Neubauer, in a personal interview with the author.
10. Judith S. Wallerstein and Joan Berlin Kelly, *Surviving the Breakup: How Children and Parents Cope with Divorce* (New York: Basic Books, 1980). The passages quoted are from pp. 83 and 306.
11. Dr. Michael I. Cohen, in a personal interview with the author, 1981.
12. *Phi Delta Kappan*, April 1980.
13. "One-Parent Families and Their Children: The Schools' Most Significant Minority—First-Year Report of a Longitudinal Study Cosponsored by the National Association of Elementary School Principals and the Institute for Development of Educational Activities," *Principal* 60 (September 1980). "Another Look at the Children of Divorce: Summary Report of the Study of School Needs of One-Parent Children," *Principal* 62 (September 1982).
14. "A Study of the School Needs of Children from One-Parent Families," *Phi Delta Kappan*, April 1980.

CHAPTER NINE. THE END OF REPRESSION

1. Haim G. Ginott, *Between Parent and Child* (New York: Macmillan, 1965).
2. Thomas Szasz, *Sex by Prescription* (New York: Doubleday Anchor Books, 1980).
3. Alex Comfort and Jane Comfort, *The Facts of Love: Living, Loving and Growing* (New York: Crown Publishers, 1979). Sex Information and Education Council of the United States (SIECUS), *Sexuality and Man* (New York: Scribner, 1970). Hal M. Wells, *The Sensuous Child* (New York: Stein & Day, 1976), p. 14.

4. Warren R. Johnson, "Childhood Sexuality: The Last of the Great Taboos," *New York SIECUS Report* 5 (March 1977).
5. Furstenberg et al., *Teenage Sexuality*, p. 78. Bruno Bettelheim, *Surviving and Other Essays* (New York: Alfred A. Knopf, 1979), p. 379.
6. Elizabeth J. Roberts, David Kline, and John Gagnon, "Family Life and Sexual Learning: A Study of the Role of Parents in the Sexual Learning of Children," prepared by the Project on Human Sexual Development, Popular Education, Inc.
7. Warren J. Gadpaille, *Cycles of Sex,* ed. Lucy Freeman (San Francisco, Calif.: W. H. Freeman, 1975).
8. Kathryn Watterson Burkhart, *Growing into Love: Teenagers Talk Candidly About Sex in the 1980's* (New York: G. P. Putnam, 1981). The quoted passages are from pp. 20, 203–5, and 215.

CHAPTER TEN. RETARDING SEXUALITY

1. Christian Miller, "A Scottish Childhood," *New Yorker,* November 12, 1979.
2. Sylvester Graham, *Chastity, A Course of Lectures for Young Men Intended Also for the Serious Consideration of Parents and Guardians* (Boston: Light & Stearns, 1837).
3. Leona Zacharias, Ph.D., and Richard Wurtman, M.D., "Average Age at Menarche," *New England Journal of Medicine* 000 (April 17, 1969); also, J. M. Tanner, "Early Maturation in Man," *Scientific American* 218 (January 1968).
4. Rose E. Frisch, "Pubertal Adipose Tissue: Is It Necessary for Normal Sexual Maturation?" *Federal Proceedings* 39 (May 15, 1980).
5. Rose E. Frisch, "Athletics Can Combat Teenage Pregnancy," letter to the editor, *New York Times,* July 16, 1981.
6. For further details, see Frank F. Furstenberg, Jr. *Unplanned Parenthood: The Social Consequences of Teenage Childbearing* (New York: Free Press, 1976).
7. *American Film Institute Catalog,* cited in Blair Justice and Rita Justice, *The Broken Taboo: Sex in the Family* (New York: Human Sciences Press, 1979).

CHAPTER ELEVEN. LATENCY AND LEARNING

1. Sigmund Freud, *Three Essays on Sexuality* (1905), *The Complete Psychologi-*

cal Works (Standard Edition), ed. and trans. James Strachey (London: Hogarth Press, 1953–66), vol. 7, p. 178.

2. S. Freud, *New Introductory Lectures in Psychoanalysis* (1933), Standard Edition, vol. 22, p. 149.

3. S. Freud, "Analysis Terminable and Interminable" (1937), Standard Edition, vol. 23, pp. 223–24.

4. Anna Freud, "Psychoanalysis and the Training of the Young Child," *Psychoanalytic Quarterly* 4 (1935), p. 20.

5. S. Freud, "The Question of Lay Analysis" (1926), Standard Edition, vol. 20, p. 217.

6. Dr. Anke Erhardt, in a personal interview with the author.

7. The Kinderheim Baumgarten experiment is discussed in Sol Cohen, "In the Name of Prevention of Neurosis: The Search for a Psychoanalytic Pedagogy in Europe, 1905–1938," in Barbara Finkelstein, ed., *Regulated Children, Liberated Children* (New York: Psychohistory Press, 1979).

CHAPTER TWELVE. PROLONGING CHILDHOOD

1. Konrad Lorenz, "Part and Parcel in Animal and Human Societies," *Studies in Animal and Human Behavior,* vol. 2 (Cambridge, Mass.: Harvard University Press, 1971).

2. Stephen Jay Gould, "A Biological Homage to Mickey Mouse," *The Panda's Thumb: More Reflections in Natural History* (New York: W. W. Norton, 1980).

3. Nan Robertson, "Wanting Children: The Factors Involved," *New York Times,* March 16, 1981.

4. B. F. Skinner, *Particulars of My Life* (New York: Alfred A. Knopf, 1976), p. 63.

5. Laurence W. Wylie, *Village in the Vaucluse,* 3rd ed. (Cambridge, Mass.: Harvard University Press, 1974).

CHAPTER THIRTEEN. THE MEANING OF CHILDHOOD

1. Mel Roman, in a personal interview with the author.

2. A. Freud, *Psychoanalysis for Teachers and Parents,* p. 32.

3. Jane Brody, Personal Health column, *New York Times,* August 11, 1982.

4. Bruno Bettelheim, *The Children of the Dream* (New York: Macmillan, 1969).

5. Mary Kohler, "The Rights of Children: An Unexplored Constituency," *Social Policy*, March–April 1971.

6. Helen Vendler, "The Music of What Happens," book review of *The Poems of Seamus Heaney*, *New Yorker*, September 28, 1981.

7. Dr. Annie Herman, in a personal interview with the author.

8. Dr. Peter Neubauer, in a personal interview with the author.

9. Dr. Annie Herman, in a personal interview with the author.

AFTERWORD. THE NEW MIDDLE AGES

1. Russell Baker, *Growing Up* (New York: Congdon & Weed, 1982), p. 42.

INDEX

*A*BOUT THE AUTHOR

Marie Winn has written eleven books, both for parents and for children, the most recent of which is *The Plug-In Drug: Television, Children, and the Family.* She is a regular contributor to the *New York Times Magazine,* and the mother of two sons: Steven Miller, a violin major at Indiana University School of Music, and Michael Miller, a Harvard student whose first book is being published this spring.